TABLE OF CONTENTS

* Note: Throughout this zoo guide, animals are listed alphabetically. However, the animals in these sections have been grouped together for easy access since most zoos have grouped many, if not all, of these animals in the same location. The animals within these sections are also listed alphabetically.

FOREWORD

Zoos are wonderful collections of many of the world's most exotic, beautiful, and unique creatures God created, but so often zoos teach the evolutionary message of millions of years and survival of the fittest. As we take our students or children to the zoo, we must be prepared to confront this evolutionary teaching with the truths of the Bible. We should be equipped with a biblical understanding of God's Word. This Zoo Guide is designed to equip you and your children or students with the biblical knowledge necessary to combat the message of these zoos.

The introductory pages of the Zoo Guide provide foundational information to help you better understand the beginning of our world and the effects of the Fall on all of creation. It also informs you on such topics as evolution, natural selection, animal kinds, and extinction from a biblical perspective. Each animal information page includes the animal's scientific classification, weight, size, diet, habitat and range information, features, fun facts, and design elements. These pages direct our attention to the Creator God and His creativity and handiwork in His creation.

This Zoo Guide provides all ages with Bible-based information that refutes the evolutionary interpretation you see at the zoo. Animals we see at the zoo are amazing testaments to God's handiwork. The Zoo Guide provides the correct perspective to these amazing creatures.

SPECIAL THANKS
- Gary and Mary Parker for their work in beginning this project and providing great information for this Zoo Guide
- Dr. Charles Jackson and Donna O'Daniel for proofing this project's accuracy

GLOSSARY

ARBOREAL Inhabiting or frequenting trees

BIOME A major living community characterized by the dominant forms of plant life and the prevailing climate, such as desert or grassland

CARCASS The dead body of an animal

CARRION Dead and decaying flesh

CARNIVORE A flesh-eating animal

CONIFEROUS Trees or shrubs bearing cones and evergreen leaves

DECIDUOUS Trees that shed or lose their leaves at the end of the growing season

DIURNAL Occurring or active during the daytime rather than at night

ECOLOGY A branch of science concerned with the interrelationship of organisms and their environments

ECOSYSTEM An ecological community together with its environment, functioning as a unit

ESTUARY The wide part of a river where it nears the sea where fresh and salt water mix

HABITAT The area or environment where an organism or ecological community normally lives

HERBIVORE An animal that feeds chiefly on plants

HOMOZYGOUS Carrying two identical copies of a gene for a given trait on the two corresponding chromosomes

INSECTIVORE An organism that feeds mainly on insects

KIND The original organisms (and their descendants) created supernaturally by God as described in Genesis 1 that reproduce only members of their own kind within the limits of pre-programmed information, but with great variation

LIGER The offspring of a male lion and a female tiger

MAMMAL Any of various warm-blooded vertebrate animals characterized by a covering of hair on the skin and, in the female, milk-producing mammary glands for nourishing the young

MARINE Native to or inhabiting the sea

MARSUPIAL Mammals of which the females have a pouch (the marsupium) where the young are fed and carried

MONOTREME An order of egg-laying mammals restricted to Australia and New Guinea and consisting of only the platypus and the echidna

NOCTURNAL Occurring or active during the night rather than in daytime

OMNIVORE An animal that feeds on both animals and plants

OVIPAROUS Producing eggs that develop and hatch outside the mother's body

PLACENTAL Mammals having a placenta—an organ that nourishes the developing young by receiving nutrients from the mother's blood and passing out waste

VIVIPAROUS Giving birth to live offspring that develop within the mother's body

INTRODUCTION

ZOOS AND THEIR UNDERLYING PHILOSOPHIES

Anticipation always accompanies a trip to the zoo. And why not? The zoo is filled with exotic animals that most people don't see every day. The zoo is a place where a child can watch and learn from the animal kingdom up close and personal. But what lessons are zoos teaching? Are they teaching the true history of each animal? In most cases, if not all, zoos teach evolution and naturalism—teachings that are not in God's Word. On exhibit plaques and brochures throughout these zoos, the teachings of evolution claim that every feature of every animal is the result of natural processes that occurred by chance. As you take your trip through the zoo, enjoy the wonders of God's creation, but be aware of the teaching that is set before your eyes and minds and the eyes and minds of your children. Zoos have their own philosophies about the origins of life, and those philosophies will be displayed throughout the zoo. Look for those philosophies, and use them to teach your children and to remind yourself of God's hand in all of nature.

DAYS OF CREATION

In Genesis 1 God tells us how and when He created everything—the animals, the stars, the moon, and man. The Bible tells us that on Day 1 God created the earth, space, time, and light. On Day 2 He separated the waters on and above the earth. On Day 3 He created dry land and all the plants. On Day 4 God created the sun, moon, and stars; and on Day 5 He created the sea animals and the birds. Day 6 was when God created the land animals and man. When God created the first man and woman, He made them different from the animals. He created Adam out of the dust of the ground and Eve out of Adam's rib. God created man and woman in His image so that they could have a relationship with their Creator God. Now, the animals that we see in the zoo probably do not look exactly like the animal kinds that God originally created on Days 5 and 6, but we will discuss that later (see Animal Kinds and Adaptations on page 8). According to the Bible, God took six days close to 6,000 years ago to create all the original kinds of plants and animals, the whole universe—the sun, moon, and stars—and Adam and Eve. Everything was perfect, and God called all He had created "very good."

THE FALL

God's creation was perfect; there was no sickness, pain, or death. But this perfect creation did not last long. God placed Adam and Eve in the Garden of Eden where they could enjoy all of His creation. God gave Adam and Eve a rule: Don't eat of the Tree of the Knowledge of Good and Evil. God told them that if they ate of it, they would die. One day Eve was walking in the Garden and the serpent spoke to her. He questioned God's goodness to Eve, and he tempted her to eat the fruit from the Tree of the Knowledge of Good and Evil. Eve ate of the fruit and disobeyed God. She then gave the fruit to Adam, and he ate. This disobedience was sin against a holy God. And since God is completely holy, He had to punish that sin. God had warned Adam and Eve that if they ate of the Tree, they would die. When God came to walk with them that day, He punished their sin. The earth was now cursed. Death was now part of life; both animals and humans would now die (Genesis 3:19; Romans 8:20–22). When the first humans sinned, it changed all of creation. The ground was cursed and would produce weeds and thorns (Genesis 3:17–18). Animals began to hunt other animals. Man would now have to work hard for food, and woman would have pain in bearing and raising her children. All mankind would now be born with a sin nature, which causes us to reject God. Adam and Eve's first sin is what we call the Fall.

DEATH

Since death was a result of the Fall, you may wonder what Adam, Eve, and the animals ate when they were first created. The answer is simple. According to God's Word, they ate plants (Genesis 1:29–30). Even though this answer sounds simple, it has caused some to wonder about the difference between plant life, animal life, and human life. The Bible says that death was a result of the Fall, but if plants died before the Fall, then death was present before sin. The difference between plant life, animal life, and human life is spoken of in the Word of God. Throughout the Bible, the Hebrew word *nephesh chayyâh* is used to describe human and animal life. When referring to mankind, *nephesh chayyâh* is often translated as "living soul." When referring to animals, it is translated "living creature." However, this word is never applied to plant life. There is a plain distinction. It is easy to see that plants do not experience pain, suffering, or death in the same way that humans and animals do. Their death is not the death of a "living soul" or "living creature." Therefore the eating of plants did not constitute death before the Fall. Possibly included with plants are the lower invertebrates, since they too were excluded from the *nephesh chayyâh* creatures. To gain a better understanding that there was no "living creature death" before the Fall of Adam, we must interpret the Bible correctly and read what God has written. God's Word plainly teaches that death is the result of sin. Therefore, there was no human or animal (*nephesh chayyâh*) death before sin.

THE FLOOD

Ever since Adam, man has continued to turn his back on his Creator and has done his own thing. The people grew so wicked that God decided to destroy the earth and everything that lived on the earth. But God knew one man who followed Him. That man was Noah. God spoke with Noah and told Noah that He was going to destroy all the earth by water—a global flood. However, God wished to spare Noah, and so He told Noah to build an Ark, which would hold his wife, his sons, their wives, and two of every kind of air-breathing, land animal and bird (and seven of some). This boat was huge. It was over 450 ft (122 m) long and 75 ft (23 m) wide. It took Noah quite a while to build his boat, but once he, his family, and the animals were on board, God closed the door. Then for 40 days and nights, the water in the atmosphere fell, and the waters in the earth came out. For 150 days water covered the whole earth, covering even the earth's highest hills by over 22 ft (7 m). And the waters remained on the earth for over a year, until Noah and his family could leave the Ark. All the people and land animals outside the Ark died. The waters were so powerful that tons of rocks and soil were moved around during the Flood. Plants, animals, and even humans became buried in this soil. Some of these bones have been dug up today; they are called fossils. Not all fossils are from the Flood, but most of them are. After the floodwaters drained into the ocean basins, the whole earth was changed—mountains, valleys, the climate ... everything.

EXTINCTION

When all members of a certain species of animal die out, it is said to have gone extinct. Extinction may occur because of changes in habitat, sickness, disease, starvation, or by hunting. Many animals have become extinct in the past and extinction can happen to any animal. One extinct animal kind (as far as we know) that everyone enjoys is the dinosaur. When talking about the dinosaurs, or any other extinct animals, we must keep some things in mind. First, we know that dinosaurs were real because the Bible says that land animals were created on Day 6, and since dinosaurs are land animals, they were included in this creation. We also know that dinosaurs were real because their bones have been discovered and preserved for us to see. Second, we must remember that when God sent the Flood to punish mankind's wickedness, God preserved his creation by sending animals onto the Ark. Dinosaurs would have also been on the Ark and preserved from the Flood. Dinosaurs could have fit on the Ark, since on average, dinosaurs are about the size of a small pony. And God would have preserved the younger dinosaur kinds to reproduce after the Flood. Third, since representatives of the dinosaur kinds were on the Ark and survived the Flood, something must have happened to them after that, which caused them to die out. There are many things that could have contributed to the extinction of the dinosaurs, including climate change, starvation, diseases, and hunting by humans and/or other animals (some of the same reasons animals today become extinct!). Finally, we should remember that some animals that were thought to have been extinct for a long time have actually been found alive and well in different parts of the world (for example, the coelacanth). So, is it possible to ever find a live dinosaur on earth again? Maybe!

ANIMAL KINDS AND ADAPTATIONS

On Days 5 and 6 God created the various animal kinds. What is an animal "kind"? Most likely, a "kind" represents a group of animals that can mate with others in that group. It is not necessarily the same grouping as the species that we use today. For example, lions, tigers, jaguars, and leopards are classified as different species, but are probably all members of an original cat kind. Also, donkeys, zebras, thoroughbreds, and Arabians are probably all part of one of the original horse kinds. What did these original kinds look like? We don't know for sure, but the representatives of each kind had enough information in their DNA to produce the wide variety of animal species that we see today. (DNA is the molecule inside the body's cells that contains the genetic information that will determine the growth and development of that organism.) For more information on the original kinds, see www.AnswersInGenesis.org/go/liger. Note: The combination of the different animal species into animal kinds is still being studied. This area of creation science is called baraminology. Throughout this guide, the animals listed in the "Created Kind Members" section of each page are ones thought to have been in the subject's created kind, but these are still tentative.

DEFENSE ATTACK STRUCTURES

The Bible tells us that before the Fall, every animal ate only plants and vegetables (Genesis 1:29–30). Death (including animal death) entered the world as a result of Adam's sin (Romans 5:12; 8:20–22). It was only after the Flood that God gave man permission to eat other things besides plants (Genesis 9:3). As you look at the animals in the zoo, you may wonder how there could be no animal death before Adam sinned, when so many animals look like they were designed to attack and eat other animals, or to defend themselves from other animals. There are several possible explanations. First, the harmful structures (like sharp teeth, poison, and claws) may have been used for different functions before the Fall and animals only began using them for attack and defense afterward. A second possibility is that the defense or attack structures may have changed into what they are today by mutations or other processes. A third option is that the animals may have been redesigned after the Fall, as part of God's curse on all of creation, including the animals (remember, the form of the serpent was changed—Genesis 3:14). And finally, it is also possible that since God foreknew the Fall would happen, the information for these structures could have been "programmed" in the first animals and that the information was "switched on" after the Fall. The most important thing to remember about the function of defense and attack structures is that they were not part of God's original creation; they came about as a result of the Curse on creation after Adam sinned.

EVOLUTION

A popular belief today is that all animals and humans evolved (changed) from one kind into another kind over millions of years. Evolution claims that everything we see happened by purely natural processes. Some believe that in the beginning God created simple life forms, and then let natural processes take over, so that what we see today evolved from these early simple life forms. Some say that there is no God who created or began anything. These people would say that everything is the result of time and natural processes, that everything happened by accident. Evolution often includes the belief that life formed from something that was not living, and then that life evolved, over millions of years, into the different animals we have today. Some evolutionists even believe that humans evolved from ape-like creatures and that dinosaurs evolved into birds. Scientists have demonstrated for us that these things are just not possible: life can't come from non-living chemicals; animals don't change into other kinds of animals. Even though evolution is taught in most public and private school textbooks, molecules-to-man evolution is not fact. It is based on the ideas of man, not on the Bible, which comes from God.

NATURAL SELECTION

Many evolutionists claim that natural selection is the process that drives evolution. However, natural selection actually works in the opposite direction of what molecules-to-man evolution requires. Evolution requires that, over time, living things must add more information to their DNA as they gain new features, abilities, or structures. However, scientists have shown us that this doesn't happen. But scientists have observed that animals reproduce "after their kind," just as the Bible teaches (dogs have puppies, cats have kittens, geese have goslings, kangaroos have joeys, etc.). Sometimes, some animals aren't born with the ability to survive in their environment. Natural selection is the process by which animals die out when they don't have the ability to adapt to their surroundings. Those animals that have the ability to adapt are able to survive and reproduce more animals like themselves. For example, many animals that live in drier regions of the world are able to gain most of the water they need from the plants they eat. Animals without this feature would have a harder time trying to survive in that region, and would eventually die out. God created the original animal kinds with much diversity in their DNA, so that as they reproduced and filled the earth, their descendants would be able to adapt to many different environments. Natural selection may bring about a new variety of animal, but cannot generate a new kind of animal.

BIOMES

The world is full of diversity. Different animals, different people groups, and different habitats make each area of the world unique. The world today is actually divided into four major biotic communities, called biomes. These biomes range in temperature and rainfall, and therefore they have very different animal and plant life. It is important to have a basic knowledge of these different biomes to better understand why certain animals live in certain regions of the world. The four major biomes are as follows: tundra, forests, grasslands, and deserts. Let's look into them a little more.

TUNDRA

The tundra region is located near the north and south poles. The subsurface land is frozen all year because of the extremely low temperatures. There is very little precipitation, and therefore very little plant life. Actually, there are no trees that grow in this region. The animals that live here have adapted to live within this cold biome.

FORESTS

Following the tundra region comes the forest. This region can actually be separated into three separate regions: coniferous forests, deciduous forests, and rainforests.

Coniferous

The coniferous forest region is also called the taiga or boreal forest. This region is closest to the tundra region and also has extremely cold temperatures, low precipitation, and forests of coniferous trees. Coniferous trees are trees that produce cones (for example, pine trees). There is limited animal and plant diversity because of the more severe temperatures. The animals in this ecosystem are either equipped to live within these temperatures, or they were designed with the knowledge and ability to migrate south during the harshest winter months.

Deciduous

Deciduous forests are filled with trees that lose their leaves during the winter months and regrow them in the spring. Within this region temperatures and precipitation vary through four seasons: spring, summer, fall, and winter. This region is home to a great diversity of plant and animal life because of its temperate climate and appropriate rainfall.

Rainforest

Most rainforests are located close to the equator where the greatest amount of rain falls. Temperatures remain high throughout the year in these tropical forests, which have the greatest variety of both plant and animal life. There are also a few temperate rainforests.

GRASSLANDS

Also known as savannas, pampas, plains, steppes, and prairies, grasslands are regions mostly located between forests and deserts. Grasses cover the grasslands, and a few trees and low shrubs dot the terrain. The temperatures vary from the hot summers to the cold winters in some locations. These areas also have short wet seasons.

DESERTS

This region is the harshest environment of all with its low rainfall and extreme temperatures. Nights are very cold, and days are very hot. Deserts, however, are mostly classified by the amount of precipitation received in a year. Arctic regions can also be classified as deserts since they too receive a small amount of precipitation. Plant and animal life is very limited in deserts, but God equipped certain animals and plants to live in this biome.

STEWARDSHIP

After God created Adam and Eve, He told them to be fruitful and multiply, and to have dominion over the creation (Genesis 1:26–28). They were to tend the Garden and to eat from its produce. They were also to care for the animals. God owns the earth (Psalm 24:1), but He has asked us to be responsible stewards of His creation (which is now suffering from the Curse). We can do this by not littering or polluting our air or water unnecessarily. Stewardship can be taken to an extreme of placing the animals over humans, but we need to be careful to avoid this mentality. Man is God's special creation, since we were created in His image (Genesis 1:26–27). Let's all do our part in being good stewards of the world that God gave us so that others can also enjoy it in the years to come.

THE GOOD NEWS

When Adam sinned, all of creation was cursed. Part of that curse on man was separation between God and man. Before the Fall, Adam and Eve had walked with God in perfect fellowship, but after the Fall, sin separated man from his Creator. And sin continues to separate us from God. God is perfect and requires those who come to live with Him to also be perfect. But since we are born with a sin nature and because we sin against God daily, we can never get to Heaven by anything that we do. And since God must punish sin as He punished Adam and Eve's sin in the Garden, our punishment is an eternity separated from God. It sounds hopeless, unless there is someone who would be willing to pay our sin penalty for us. That someone must be without sin—perfect. Jesus, the Son of God, is that perfect God-man who took upon Himself the penalty for our sin. Jesus died on a cross, paying for our sin; and three days later He rose again, defeating death to provide us with a way to one day live with Him. But for us to be acceptable to God, we must repent of our sins and place our faith in Jesus. We must believe that Jesus took our place on the Cross and died for us. Even though some people say that there are many ways to God, there is actually only one way. Jesus said in John 14:6, "I am the way, the truth, and the life. No one comes to the Father except through me." Jesus is our only way to be reconciled with God. We can never earn eternal life on our own, because of our sin. Jesus paid our penalty and made a way for us to live with Him forever. We must repent of our sin and place our trust in Him—that is the good news.

ANTELOPE

ANTELOPE
CREATED ON DAY 6

DESIGN

The hooves of the antelope vary greatly between species. One species, *Tragelaphus spekeii*, has wide hooves because it lives in the wetlands, while the *Oreotragus oreotragus* has a pad in the center of its tiny, rounded hooves because it lives in rocky regions. The hooves of the different species of antelope demonstrate how God equipped them to live in different habitats.

FEATURES

- All antelopes have horns that are permanently attached. Some horns are twisted in spirals, others have ridges, and others grow in wide curves.

FUN FACTS

- Antelopes are powerful swimmers. If threatened, some species will jump in and hide under the water's surface, with only their noses sticking out.
- Another species of antelope attracts a mate by repeatedly sticking out its tongue. It uses this same technique to ward off enemies.
- If an antelope gets separated from the rest of the group, it can find them by smelling the scent trail that the herd left behind from the scent glands on their hooves.

CREATED KIND MEMBERS

Impala, wildebeest, gazelle

CLASS:	Mammalia (mammal)
ORDER:	Artiodactyla (even-toed)
FAMILY:	Bovidae (cloven-hooves; two-toed)
GENUS/SPECIES:	There are over 90 species of antelope
Size:	Largest antelope: up to 11 ft long (3.3 m); Smallest: around 19 in long (0.5 m)
Weight:	Range from about 5 lbs to 2,000 lbs (2–900 kg)
Original Diet:	Plants
Present Diet:	Mostly herbivorous (plant-eating)
Habitat:	Open plains in Africa, Asia, the Middle East, and Eastern Europe (based on species)

ARCTIC FOX

ARCTIC FOX
CREATED ON DAY 6

DESIGN
Since the arctic fox inhabits the tundra, it possesses a fine undercoat that is thick and dense, and small ears to save body heat. This undercoat insulates its body from the freezing temperatures of the region. The arctic fox has two color phases: white and a bluish gray. The white phase is brown to brownish-gray in the summer and almost pure white in the winter. The blue phase is chocolate brown in the summer and lighter brown tinged with a blue sheen in the winter.

FEATURES
- The arctic fox is also known as the polar fox or the white fox.
- The arctic fox is distinctive because of its furred paws. It has short legs, a short muzzle, and short ears.

FUN FACTS
- Generations of foxes may use the same dens.
- The arctic fox has the most offspring in a litter, up to 25 at one time. That's the largest litter size of all carnivores.

CREATED KIND MEMBERS
Jackal, wolf, dingo, coyote, domesticated dog

CLASS: Mammalia (mammal)
ORDER: Carnivora (meat-eating)
FAMILY: Canidae (dog kind)
GENUS/SPECIES: *Alopex lagopus*

Size: Average 43 in (1.1 m)
Weight: 6–10 lbs (2.7–4.5 kg)
Original Diet: Plants
Present Diet: Prefers small mammals, but will also eat vegetation and dead animals
Habitat: Arctic tundra in both Old and New World

ARMADILLO

ARMADILLO
CREATED ON DAY 6

DESIGN

Since the armadillo is almost blind, God equipped it with an excellent sense of smell and good hearing so it can locate food and escape predators. The armadillo can store enough oxygen to allow it to stop breathing for up to 6 minutes. This allows it to float across rivers and survive flash floods. It can also cross rivers by holding its breath and walking along the bottom. The armadillo is able to live in regions with hot days and cold nights because of its wonderfully-designed heating system. This system allows heat to be transferred from the arteries right to the veins without going to the legs first.

FEATURES

- The small body of the armadillo is almost completely surrounded by many strong bony plates (tail included in most species).
- It has a long, sticky tongue used to capture insects.

FUN FACTS

- Most armadillos cannot roll up into balls, as many people have believed. Their plates prevent it. (Only one species can since its shell is divided into three sections giving it "flexibility").
- Some armadillos can jump as high as 3 ft (1 m) straight up to confuse or avoid predators.
- Most armadillos have a litter of four young—two males and two females.

CREATED KIND MEMBERS

Six-banded armadillo, long-nosed armadillo, giant armadillo, fairy armadillo

CLASS:	Mammalia (mammal)
ORDER:	Xenarthra (strange-jointed)
FAMILY:	Dasypodidae (armadillos)
GENUS/SPECIES:	Close to 30 species
Size:	6 in–5 ft (0.2 m–1.5 m) depending on species
Weight:	0.2–110 lbs (0.1–50 kg) depending on species
Original Diet:	Plants
Present Diet:	Insects and plants
Habitat:	Central and South America and Texas in open fields and near forests

BADGER

BADGER
CREATED ON DAY 6

DESIGN

Badgers eat many small mammals and pests that can quickly overpopulate areas. They were originally created as vegetarians, but after the Fall, they became helpful in keeping the populations of many of these animals from becoming too large. The excellent senses of hearing and smell let the badger find food that is underground.

FEATURES

- The badger's body is wide and relatively flat-looking.

FUN FACTS

- The badger seems unharmed by the venom of rattlesnakes, unless bitten on the nose.
- The skin of the badger is very loose-fitting which allows it to sometimes break free from a predator's hold.
- The badger has been known to plug the exit holes of its prey before attempting to capture it.
- The home of the badger—underground tunnels and chambers—is called a sett.

CREATED KIND MEMBERS

Weasel, otter, wolverine, ferret

CLASS:	Mammalia (mammal)
ORDER:	Carnivora (meat-eating)
FAMILY:	Mustelidae (weasels, otters, badgers)
GENUS/SPECIES:	There are 56 different species of badger
Size:	Between 30 and 35 in (0.8–0.9 m)
Weight:	12–16 lbs (5.4–7.3 kg)
Original Diet:	Plants
Present Diet:	Squirrels, gophers, rats, and mice, as well as birds and snakes
Habitat:	Edge of forests and open plains, mainly found in Canada, North America, and Europe

BAT

BAT
CREATED ON DAY 5

DESIGN

God designed bats with an effective echolocation system with which they locate and even identify their prey. This system is far superior to man-made systems such as radar and sonar. A bat can identify its own sound even among thousands of other bat signals. All fossils of bats are essentially no different from bats found today. This shows that since God created them, the bat has not changed, or changed only slightly.

FEATURES

- Bats are the only truly flying mammals and are in an order all their own.
- Their powerful feet are able to hold their body weight while hanging upside down.

FUN FACTS

- One insectivorous bat can consume over 600 mosquitoes in a single hour.
- Bats live in huge colonies, some numbering in the millions.
- Fruit and nectar-eating bats are important seed dispersers and plant/tree pollinators of our tropical rainforests.

CREATED KIND MEMBERS

Big brown bat, silver-haired bat, Mexican free-tailed bat, pipistrelle bat

CLASS:	Mammalia (mammal)
ORDER:	Chiroptera (hand wings)
FAMILY:	18 families
GENUS/SPECIES:	More than 1,000 different species
Size:	Largest wingspan: over 6 ft (2 m)
	Smallest wingspan: around 6 in (0.2 m)
Weight:	Varies based on species from 0.5 oz to 3 lbs (0.01–1.4 kg)
Original Diet:	Plants
Present Diet:	Mostly fruits, nectar, and insects; also reptiles and fish; the vampire bat drinks the blood of vertebrate animals
Habitat:	Rainforests, temperate forests, urban areas, and deserts; all continents except Antarctica

BEAVER

BEAVER
CREATED ON DAY 6

DESIGN

God created the beaver with valves that close off its ears and nostrils when it dives underwater. It also has a skin flap that seals off its mouths but leaves its incisors exposed for use while underwater. This animal also has transparent eyelids. These not only allow the beaver to see well underwater, but they also protect the eyes from debris. For a beaver to be an efficient diver, its heart is designed to beat more slowly during a dive. This conserves oxygen and keeps the blood supply to the brain normal.

FEATURES

- Most beaver species are recognized by the large flat, paddle-shaped tail.
- It has large, webbed hind feet for digging and swimming.

FUN FACTS

- The beaver is the largest rodent in North America.
- It uses its tail to warn others of the presence of predators, to swim, and to stand upright. It does not use it to build dams.
- The beavers stores branches of trees on the bottom of ponds for winter food.

CREATED KIND MEMBERS

American beaver, giant beaver

CLASS:	Mammalia (mammal)
ORDER:	Rodentia (rodents)
FAMILY:	Castoridae (beavers)
GENUS/SPECIES:	*Castor canadensis* and *C. fiber* (American and Eurasian)
Size:	3–4 ft (0.9–1.2 m) long, including the tail
Weight:	Between 30 and 70 lbs (14–32 kg)
Original Diet:	Plants
Present Diet:	Plants, bark, and roots of trees
Habitat:	Forested stream systems in North America, Northern Europe, and Northern Asia

BLACK BEAR

BLACK BEAR
CREATED ON DAY 6

DESIGN

God designed the female black bear with something called "delayed implantation," when her fertilized eggs do not begin to develop until the fall. Delayed implantation gives bear cubs the best chance to survive the winter since they are born in the protection of the den while the mother bear hibernates. As the cub grows, the mother must teach necessary survival behaviors.

FEATURES

- The black bear looks different from the brown bear with its longer and less furry ears, smaller shoulder humps, and rounder profile.
- The black bear is an inquisitive animal, sometimes searching out human domains in search of food.

FUN FACTS

- The black bear is not a social creature. Males and females are only found together during mating season.
- At birth, a black bear cub weighs less than a pound (0.5 kg).
- Even though this animal appears ferocious, it is mainly vegetarian.

CREATED KIND MEMBERS

Brown bear, panda, polar bear

CLASS:	Mammalia (mammal)
ORDER:	Carnivora (meat-eating)
FAMILY:	Ursidae (bear kind)
GENUS/SPECIES:	*Ursus americanus* and *U. thibetanus* (American and Asian)
Size:	Male: 4–6.5 ft (1.4–2 m); Female: 4–5.3 ft (1.2–1.6 m)
Weight:	Male: 100–900 lbs (47–409 kg); Female: 85–520 lbs (39–236 kg)
Original Diet:	Plants
Present Diet:	Fruits and vegetation, mainly; also small animals and insects; they will also consume garbage
Habitat:	North America and parts of Mexico

BROWN BEAR

BROWN BEAR
CREATED ON DAY 6

DESIGN

During the winter months when vegetation and animal life is scarcer, the brown bear goes into hibernation. It is during this state that its body temperature drops and its metabolic rate decreases, allowing it to survive on less food. The female brown bear is a very protective mother, and will attack humans if its cubs are endangered.

FEATURES

- The brown bear has small ears and high shoulders. It can range in color from cinnamon to almost black.
- It is also known as the Kodiak bear.

FUN FACTS

- The grizzly bear is included as a subspecies of the brown bear. The grizzly gets its name from its appearance. As it ages, the tips of its guard hairs turn silvery-gray.
- A brown bear can eat 25–35 lbs (11–16 kg) of food a day.
- It is the second largest bear in the world—the polar bear being the largest.
- Over 98% of the brown bear population in the U.S. is found in Alaska.

CREATED KIND MEMBERS

Black bear, panda, polar bear

CLASS:	Mammalia (mammal)
ORDER:	Carnivora (meat-eating)
FAMILY:	Ursidae (bear kind)
GENUS/SPECIES:	*Ursus arctos*
Size:	Nearly 6 ft to over 9 ft tall (1.7–2.8 m)
Weight:	209–1,700 lbs (95–771 kg)
Original Diet:	Plants
Present Diet:	Plants, fish, and other animals; a favorite is salmon
Habitat:	Prefers the mountain forests and cold tundra in North America

CALIFORNIA SEA LION

CALIFORNIA SEA LION
CREATED ON DAY 5

DESIGN

Sea lions use a system of echolocation to navigate while underwater and to find food. A mother will leave her newborn pup while she goes hunting. To relocate each other, they will "bark" until they find each other. The mother will then smell the pup to completely identify the pup as her own. This is a unique ability designed by God. While underwater, the sea lion can open its mouth to capture prey without swallowing water. This is possible because of special muscles that close off the nostrils, larynx, and esophagus.

FEATURES

- The sea lion has a brownish coat with lighter coloring on its belly and sides.
- It has front flippers as well as two back flippers. These flippers are all coated with short, dark stubble.

FUN FACTS

- The sea lion can be easily trained which makes it a great attraction at circuses and aquariums.
- The California sea lion has been known to "adopt" an abandoned pup.
- This species can rotate its hind flippers underneath its body to help it walk on land.
- It can sleep while floating in the water.

CREATED KIND MEMBERS

Northern fur seal

CLASS:	Mammalia (mammal)
ORDER:	Carnivora (meat-eating)
FAMILY:	Otariidae (eared seals)
GENUS/SPECIES:	*Zalophus californianus*
Size:	Almost 8 ft (2.4 m)
Weight:	Up to 860 lbs (390 kg)
Original Diet:	Plants
Present Diet:	Fish and mollusks
Habitat:	Marine, in three temperate areas (west coast of North America, Galapagos Islands, and southern Sea of Japan)

CAMEL

CAMEL
CREATED ON DAY 6

DESIGN

A camel has two sets of eyelashes that protect its eyes from the blowing sands of the deserts. A camel can allow its body temperature to reach up to 106°F (41°C), which allows it to travel in hot, dry areas without losing great amounts of water. The humps of camels are not used for water-storage; they are areas of fat, which provide food during shortage. They can store up to 100 lbs (45 kg) of food. A camel's feet are specially padded to endure the hot sand of the desert without blistering.

FEATURES

- The most prominent difference between the Bactrian and Dromedary camels is their humps. The Bactrian camel has two humps on its back while the Dromedary camel has only one.
- Another difference between these two species is the length of their hair. Dromedary camels have shorter hair than the Bactrian.

FUN FACTS

- Camels are called "ships of the desert."
- A camel can consume up to 30 gallons (114 ℓ) of water at one time.
- It can close its nostrils to keep out sand.

CREATED KIND MEMBERS

Llama

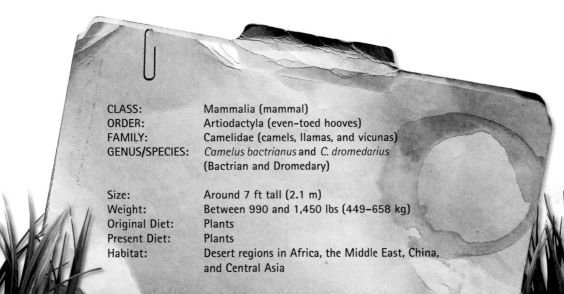

CLASS:	Mammalia (mammal)
ORDER:	Artiodactyla (even-toed hooves)
FAMILY:	Camelidae (camels, llamas, and vicunas)
GENUS/SPECIES:	*Camelus bactrianus* and *C. dromedarius* (Bactrian and Dromedary)
Size:	Around 7 ft tall (2.1 m)
Weight:	Between 990 and 1,450 lbs (449–658 kg)
Original Diet:	Plants
Present Diet:	Plants
Habitat:	Desert regions in Africa, the Middle East, China, and Central Asia

COYOTE

COYOTE
CREATED ON DAY 6

DESIGN

A coyote will sometimes hunt larger prey with other coyotes and with badgers. When hunting with a badger, the coyote will sniff out underground prey, and the badger will dig it up with its claws. How do coyotes know to hunt with badgers? God designed this instinct that became part of its behavior after the Fall of man since before this time, it was vegetarian.

FEATURES

- Most coyotes are grayish or yellowish gray in color. The guard hair on their backs is black-tipped. They have large pointed, erect ears, and small, black noses.

FUN FACTS

- Coyotes are sometimes called "song dogs" because they are the most vocal dogs.
- They howl to keep the pack together. If one gets separated, the pack will howl to help the other locate them.
- The tail of a coyote is half of the coyote's length.

CREATED KIND MEMBERS

Jackal, wolf, dingo, fox, domesticated dog

CLASS:	Mammalia (mammal)
ORDER:	Carnivora (meat-eating)
FAMILY:	Canidae (dog kind)
GENUS/SPECIES:	*Canis latrans*
Size:	2–3 ft (0.6–0.9 m)
Weight:	15–46 lbs (6.8–20.9 kg)
Original Diet:	Plants
Present Diet:	Mostly rodents; also birds, snakes, and insects
Habitat:	Desert, forest, savanna, and tundra regions of North and Central America

DINGO

DINGO
CREATED ON DAY 6

DESIGN

Dingoes can breed successfully with domesticated dogs, indicating that they are undoubtedly both members of the same original dog kind as created by God on Day Six of Creation Week. Indeed, when the European settlers first arrived in Australia, they discovered that many of the "wild dogs" were not truly "wild," but instead were kept by their Aboriginal human keepers and used as bed warmers, hunting companions, and guard dogs.

FEATURES

- Typically, the dingo's color is a variation of brown and black with white patterns.
- The dingo is commonly referred to as a wild dog.

FUN FACTS

- The dingo is not afraid of humans and is most likely to settle close to villages to avoid predators that will not approach human habitation.
- It usually hunts at night, either alone or with its other family members.
- The dingo gives birth once a year to four or five pups, in a cave or hollow log.

CREATED KIND MEMBERS

Jackal, wolf, coyote, fox, domesticated dog

CLASS:	Mammalia (mammals)
ORDER:	Carnivora (meat-eating)
FAMILY:	Canidae (dog kind)
GENUS/SPECIES:	*Canis lupus dingo*
Size:	Average 3–4 ft (0.9–1.2 m)
Weight:	Average 32 lbs (14.5 kg)
Original Diet:	Plants
Present Diet:	Mostly mammals; also birds and reptiles
Habitat:	Deserts and forests in Australia and Southeast Asia

ELEPHANT

ELEPHANT
CREATED ON DAY 6

DESIGN

Since the elephant uses its trunk for numerous reasons, God designed it with over 100,000 muscle units. This powerful tool can uproot trees, dig pits to find water, and even cripple an attacker. It can also perform very gentle tasks, like picking up berries and small leaves. Elephants also use their trunks to suck up water and dust. They drink or clean themselves with water. They blow the dust over their backs to protect them from the sun and insects. The elephant's large ears help cool the animal by providing a wide surface area for heat to escape the body and by fanning its body.

FEATURES

- African elephants are larger than Asian elephants and they even have larger ears and tusks. The head of the African elephant is tapered in the middle in comparison to the dome-shaped Asian elephant's head.
- Both male and female elephants have tusks (all except the Asian female).

FUN FACTS

- Elephants have the largest nose in the world. It has the capacity to hold 6 gallons (23 ℓ) of water.
- Elephants are either right-tusked or left-tusked, just as humans are right- or left-handed.

CREATED KIND MEMBERS

Extinct mammoths and mastodons

CLASS:	Mammalia (mammal)
ORDER:	Proboscidea (elephant)
FAMILY:	Elephantidae
GENUS/SPECIES:	*Elephas maximus* and *Loxodonta africana* (Asian and African)
Size:	African: 13 ft (4 m) tall; Asian: 8–11 ft (2.5–3.5 m) tall
Weight:	African: 7–8 tons (4,500–7,500 kg); Asian: 2–5 tons (2,000–5,000 kg)
Original Diet:	Plants
Present Diet:	Plants
Habitat:	Mostly the savannas of Africa and the tropical forests and plains of Asia

FERRET

FERRET
CREATED ON DAY 6

DESIGN

God designed ferrets to be flexible, which allows them to fully turn around while in their underground burrows. Ferrets also make good pets since they can be trained to do tricks and to use a litter box. They can also be friendly with other domestic animals, like dogs and cats.

FEATURES

- The ferret has a long, flexible body, short limbs, and a good set of teeth.
- The eyes of the black-footed ferret are surrounded by a dark mask outlined in white, while the rest of the ferret is relatively dark with a light undercoat.
- Some ferrets are completely white. Some of these albinos have black eyes while the eyes of others are pink.

FUN FACTS

- Queen Elizabeth of England had a pet ferret; you can find her portrait in Krakow, Poland that pictures her with her ferret. The painting was done by Leonardo da Vinci.
- Ferrets have the ability to spray their attackers, similar to the skunk.

CREATED KIND MEMBERS

Weasel, otter, wolverine, badger

CLASS:	Mammalia (mammal)
ORDER:	Carnivora (meat-eating)
FAMILY:	Mustelidae (weasel kind)
GENUS/SPECIES:	*Mustela putorius putorius* and *M. nigripes* (European and black-footed)
Size:	16–28 in (0.4–0.7 m)
Weight:	About 0.5–4 lbs (0.2–1.8 kg)
Original Diet:	Plants
Present Diet:	Rodents, rabbits, insects, lizards, and frogs
Habitat:	Prairies and marshes

GIANT ANTEATER

GIANT ANTEATER
CREATED ON DAY 6

DESIGN

The anteater is important to the area where it lives. Since it dines on termites and other harmful insects, the anteater keeps these colonies in check. It is also an interesting animal to look at with its unusual and distinct features. The giant anteater is designed with the ability to smell 40 times better than a human. It uses its keen sense of smell to locate food.

FEATURES

- The anteater walks on its knuckles with its toes pointed to the sides.
- It has powerful forearms and sharp claws that it uses to rip open termite and ant nests.
- The giant anteater does not have teeth while the other two species have small rudimentary teeth that are fragile and soft.

FUN FACTS

- The anteater has a tongue that can reach almost 2 ft (0.6 m).
- This animal sleeps as many as 15 hours a day. It sleeps during the day and hunts for food at night.

CREATED KIND MEMBERS

Tamandua, silky anteater

CLASS:	Mammalia (mammal)
ORDER:	Xenarthra (strange-jointed)
FAMILY:	Myrmecophagidae (anteaters)
GENUS/SPECIES:	*Myrmecophaga tridactyla*
Size:	6–8 ft (1.8–2.40 m)
Weight:	Males: 40–90 lbs (20–40 kg); Females are smaller than males
Original Diet:	Plants and insects
Present Diet:	Insects such as termites, ants, and beetles
Habitat:	Grasslands and tropical forests in central South America

GIANT PANDA

GIANT PANDA
CREATED ON DAY 6

DESIGN

Unlike other bears, the panda has enlarged wrist bones, which actually act like extra fingers for it to grasp and break tough bamboo shoots. Its jaws, teeth, esophagus, and stomach are also designed to help it eat bamboo. The esophagus is lined with a tough lining that protects the bear from splinters, and the stomach is lined with muscle to protect it.

FEATURES

- The panda is known for its distinct black and white coloring. The eyes, ears, arms, legs, and shoulders are all black while the rest of the body is white.
- The giant panda has an extra opposable digit on the hand, known as "the panda's thumb." It is actually a pad of skin covering the wrist bone.

FUN FACTS

- A baby panda weighs less than a pound at birth.
- The panda is a pretty good acrobat, enjoying somersaults.
- A pandas eats over 80 lbs (36 kg) of food a day to get all the nutrients it needs.
- Infant pandas are born with their eyes closed and they only open them when at least three weeks old. They cannot move around on their own until 3–4 months of age.

CREATED KIND MEMBERS

Brown bear, black bear, polar bear

CLASS:	Mammalia (mammal)
ORDER:	Carnivora (meat-eating)
FAMILY:	Ursidae (bear kind)
GENUS/SPECIES:	*Ailuropoda melanoleuca*
Size:	4–6 ft (1.2–1.8 m)
Weight:	175–325 lbs (79–150 kg); Males are larger than females
Original Diet:	Plants
Present Diet:	Bamboo
Habitat:	Mountain forests and mixed coniferous and broadleaf forests where bamboo is present in China

GIRAFFE

GIRAFFE
CREATED ON DAY 6

DESIGN

The giraffe is amazingly designed. The unique design of its lungs, heart, capillaries, and birth process all play vital roles in the giraffe's survival. The heart has to pump enough blood into the giraffe's brain while the capillaries have to prevent the high blood pressure from affecting the animal when it bends over to get a drink. The lungs, which are eight times the size of a human's, provide enough oxygen to the brain. The giraffe gives birth while standing up. Such a fall would mean certain death to the newborn except for the fact that the mother lowers its young to the ground slowly through use of the after-birth.

FEATURES

- The giraffe is the tallest animal in the world.
- Each giraffe has a specific set of markings unlike any other giraffe.
- The giraffe has two or three "horns" on its head called ossicones.

FUN FACTS

- The giraffe has only seven vertebrae in its long neck.
- A giraffe's heart is over 25 lbs (11 kg) which allows it to pump blood all the way up its long neck.
- The giraffe actually has the longest tail—almost 8 ft (2.4 m)—of any mammal.

CREATED KIND MEMBERS

Okapi

CLASS:	Mammalia (mammal)
ORDER:	Artiodactyla (even-toed hooves)
FAMILY:	Giraffidae (giraffes and okapis)
GENUS/SPECIES:	*Giraffa camelopardalis*
Size:	Up to 14–18 ft (4.3–5.5 m) tall
Weight:	Males: 3,000 lbs (1,360 kg); Females: 1,500 lbs (680 kg)
Original Diet:	Plants
Present Diet:	The leaves of the mimosa and acacia trees
Habitat:	Savannas of Africa

GRANT'S GAZELLE

GRANT'S GAZELLE
CREATED ON DAY 6

DESIGN

The belly of the gazelle is the perfect color to reflect the heat of the sun's rays away from the body. The gazelle was also designed with the ability to cool down its body by panting rapidly. The blood is cooled when it passes through the vessels that are in the nasal passages. This cooled blood then goes to the brain. These features were given to the gazelle by its Creator.

FEATURES

- Grant's gazelle is one of the largest in the gazelle kind.
- This gazelle is recognized from other species by the white stripes on its face that are framed in black.

FUN FACTS

- Grant's gazelles can "pronk." Pronking is the ability of these animals to leap straight up into the air and land on all four feet at once. It is not known for sure why they pronk, but the action shows great strength and stamina.
- An hour after being born, a Grant's gazelle is able to walk.
- Grant's gazelles have a life expectancy of approximately 11 years.

CREATED KIND MEMBERS

Yak, wildebeest, antelope

CLASS:	Mammalia (mammal)
ORDER:	Artiodactyla (even-toed hooves)
FAMILY:	Bovidae (antelope, cattle, gazelle, sheep, goats, and relatives)
GENUS/SPECIES:	*Gazelle granti*
Size:	5–6 ft (1.5–1.8 m) tall; over 5 ft (1.5 m) long
Weight:	Male average: 140 lbs (65 kg); Female average: 100 lbs (45 kg)
Original Diet:	Plants
Present Diet:	Plants
Habitat:	Savannas of Africa

GRAY WOLF

GRAY WOLF
CREATED ON DAY 6

DESIGN

The gray wolf has a layer of dense underfur that insulates it against the cold temperatures of its habitat. When a female gray wolf digs its den, it digs downward, then upward to prevent flooding. This instinct was given to the wolf by its Creator.

FEATURES

- Gray wolves can vary in color from white to dark gray based on where they are found.
- A gray wolf usually carries its tail high, whereas a coyote usually carries its tail below the level of the back.

FUN FACTS

- The entire wolf pack takes care of the pups. They feed and protect them.
- Wolves communicate through howling, rubbing chins, and rolling over on their backs. These motions can communicate dominance in the pack, boundaries of a pack's territory, or a call to join in a hunt.

CREATED KIND MEMBERS

Jackal, coyote, dingo, fox, domesticated dog

CLASS:	Mammalia (mammal)
ORDER:	Carnivora (meat-eating)
FAMILY:	Canidae (dog kind)
GENUS/SPECIES:	*Canis lupus*
Size:	Between 3 and 6 ft (0.9–1.8 m), with a tail of 14–22 in (0.4–0.6 m)
Weight:	50–115 lbs (23–52 kg); Males are larger than females
Original Diet:	Plants
Present Diet:	Mammals such as deer, moose, squirrels; birds and fish
Habitat:	Arctic coast of Alaska and western Canada

HIPPOPOTAMUS

HIPPOPOTAMUS
CREATED ON DAY 6

DESIGN

Hippos are very neighborly. They let birds perch on their heads and backs. These birds pick flies, ticks, and other pesky insects off the hippo. Fish also eat algae off the hippo's skin. These actions keep the hippo healthy. Hippos were designed with the ability to excrete a liquid from their pores, which protects their skin from the sun and possible infection.

FEATURES

- The hippo is known for its massive size.
- Its nostrils and eyes protrude from its head so that it can see and breathe while the rest of its body is submerged.

FUN FACTS

- The hippo can open its mouth almost 150° wide.
- Because of its great size, a hippo can actually walk or run on the bottom of the river.
- The thick layer of blubber under the hippo's skin helps it conserve body heat as it spends so much time in the water. It also makes it more buoyant.
- The hippo's eyes, ears, and nostrils are in a line along the top of its head, allowing it to breathe, see, and hear things above the water while almost totally submerged.

CREATED KIND MEMBERS

Pygmy hippopotamus

CLASS:	Mammalia (mammal)
ORDER:	Artiodactyla (even-toed hooves)
FAMILY:	Hippopotamidae (hippopotamus)
GENUS/SPECIES:	*Hippopotamus amphibious* and *Choeropsis liberiensis* (hippo and pygmy hippo)
Size:	Average 5 ft (1.5 m) tall and (11 ft (3.4 m) long
Weight:	2,500–9,000 lbs (1,135–4,080 kg)
Original Diet:	Plants
Present Diet:	Plants
Habitat:	Rivers and lakes in the savanna of Africa

JACKAL

JACKAL
CREATED ON DAY 6

DESIGN

Many jackals live in family units, with the older siblings living and helping with the younger pups. This helps protect the family. A female jackal will change its home every two weeks to protect her young from predators. This instinct became part of her behavior after the Fall when animals began hunting other animals.

FEATURES

- Two species of jackals are tan-colored while the black-backed has black hair on its back against its reddish body. Most jackals have black-tipped tails as well.

FUN FACTS

- Jackals use their tails to communicate to others. Jackals are also very noisy; they howl and yelp.
- The black-backed jackal gives birth to her young underground in an empty burrow.
- A single 20-lb (9-kg) jackal will drive off an 80-lb (36-kg) hyena.
- Jackals help keep the numbers of vermin down, such as rodents and insects, which eat crops.

CREATED KIND MEMBERS

Coyote, wolf, dingo, fox, domesticated dog

CLASS:	Mammalia (mammal)
ORDER:	Carnivora (meat-eating)
FAMILY:	Canidae (dog kind)
GENUS/SPECIES:	*Canis aureus, C. adustus,* and *C. mesomelas* (golden, side-striped, and black-backed jackal)
Size:	15–20 in (0.4–0.5 m) tall
Weight:	15–35 lbs (6.8–15.9 kg)
Original Diet:	Plants
Present Diet:	Both plants and animals; known also as a scavenger
Habitat:	Grasslands, woodlands, and deserts of Africa; one species from Arabia to India

KANGAROO

KANGAROO
CREATED ON DAY 6

DESIGN

Kangaroos are marsupials, and for the undeveloped young to survive it must immediately crawl into the mother's pouch from the birth canal, using its forearms. At this time, its hind limbs are not fully developed. The kangaroo's fur is dense, providing insulation against the heat of the sun and the cold nights. Its tail is used for balance while leaping for supporting the animal's weight, and as a prop so the hind legs can be used to defend from predators. Another amazing design is that a kangaroo embryo can remain dormant until either the pouch becomes unoccupied or the joey in the pouch dies.

FEATURES

- Males are two to three times larger than females.
- The two species are separated by their color. Western grays have darker faces and patchier coloring compared to the eastern gray.

FUN FACTS

- Kangaroos like to box. Young kangaroos do this as play while adult males use this action to show dominance.
- When they feel threatened, kangaroos will growl like a dog and stamp their hind feet on the ground.
- The kangaroo's pouch is sealed off by a series of strong muscles, protecting the joey from bouncing out or drowning when the mother goes swimming.

CREATED KIND MEMBERS

Wallaby

CLASS:	Mammalia (mammal)
ORDER:	Diprotodontia (pair of incisors on lower jaw)
FAMILY:	Macropodidae (kangaroos and wallabies)
GENUS/SPECIES:	*Macropus fuliginosus* and *M. giganteus* (western and eastern grays)
Size:	6–7 ft (1.8–2.1 m) tall
Weight:	Males: 120–200 lbs (54–90 kg); females: about 65 lbs (30 kg)
Original Diet:	Plants
Present Diet:	Plants
Habitat:	Grasslands, savannas, and open woodlands in Australia and Tasmania

KOALA

KOALA
CREATED ON DAY 6

DESIGN

The koala was designed with an opposable index finger that it uses as a second thumb for feeding and climbing. It was also designed with a padded tail, which allows it to sit in a tree all day. A koala hardly ever needs to drink water since it receive most of its water from the eucalyptus leaves that it eats. The name koala means "no-drink animal." Since the koala does not have any sweat glands, it will lick its arms and stretch out on its tree to cool off.

FEATURES

- The koala has dense fur that is colored from gray to a reddish-brown. Many also have white patches on the chest, chin, and rump.
- The pouch opens in the rear and extends upward and forward.
- The koala is completely arboreal.

FUN FACTS

- The koala is not a bear; it is a marsupial.
- It spends up to 18 hours a day sleeping.
- A koala will sometimes eat dirt. This helps it digest its food.

CREATED KIND MEMBERS

None

CLASS:	Mammalia (mammal)
ORDER:	Diprotodontia (pair of incisors on lower jaw)
FAMILY:	Phascolarctidae
GENUS/SPECIES:	*Phascolarctos cinereus*
Size:	Between 25 and 33 in (0.7–0.8 m)
Weight:	Between 15 and 30 lbs (6.8–14 kg)
Original Diet:	Plants
Present Diet:	Eucalyptus leaves, young bark, and mistletoe
Habitat:	Eucalyptus forests of eastern Australia

LLAMA

LLAMA
CREATED ON DAY 6

DESIGN

The llama has a four-chambered stomach, which allows it to chew the cud twice to gain all the nutrition it can from its food. The unique shape of the llama's red blood cells allows it to dwell in very high altitudes. Some believe the camel to have evolved from the llama; however, these two animals are probably from the same animal kind created on Day 6 of Creation Week.

FEATURES

- The llama is known for its woolly coat, which comes in a variety of brown shades, and may be 3–8 in (7.5–20 cm) in length.
- The llama has a long, graceful neck and a relatively small head with large eyes and ears.

FUN FACTS

- Llamas do spit, but only at humans when they are upset. They will spit at other llamas when deciding who gets a meal or who is more dominant.
- They are stubborn animals. They will stop, sit, or lie down if a burden is too heavy for them to carry.
- Female llamas will often hum to their offspring.

CREATED KIND MEMBERS

Camel, alpaca

CLASS:	Mammalia (mammal)
ORDER:	Artiodactyla (even-toed hooves)
FAMILY:	Camelidae (camels, llamas, and vicunas)
GENUS/SPECIES:	*Lama glama*
Size:	5–6 ft tall (1.5–1.8 m)
Weight:	150–450 lbs (68–204 kg)
Original Diet:	Plants
Present Diet:	Plants
Habitat:	South American mountains; but they are now mostly domesticated animals.

MANATEE

MANATEE
CREATED ON DAY 5

DESIGN

Manatees have an incredible immune system. They are able to heal after great injury, even injuries caused by boats. These animals have a very sensitive pattern of whiskers on their snouts for sensing their food supply in the dark, murky waters where they live.

FEATURES

- Manatees are often referred to as sea cows.
- The manatee is a large creature with two fore-flippers and one rear flipper that acts as a rudder when it swims.

FUN FACTS

- The manatee has no incisors; it only has molars, which it uses to grind vegetation.
- A manatee can weigh between 60 and 70 lbs (27–32 kg) at birth.
- Manatees are the largest of all freshwater animals.
- Continued protection of the manatee is important considering Florida's rapid growth of human population and boating traffic.

CREATED KIND MEMBERS

Florida manatee, Amazonian manatee

CLASS:	Mammalia (mammal)
ORDER:	Sirenia (mammals living in water)
FAMILY:	Trichechidae (manatees)
GENUS/SPECIES:	*Trichechus inunguis, T. senegalensis,* and *T. manatus* (Amazonian, African, and West Indian)
Size:	Average 10 ft (3 m)
Weight:	Up to 2,200 lbs (998 kg)
Original Diet:	Plants
Present Diet:	Plants
Habitat:	Aquatic, in sub-tropical and tropical areas

MEERKAT

MEERKAT
CREATED ON DAY 6

DESIGN
The meerkat was designed with the ability to close its ears. This is helpful as it burrows in the dry dirt. The fur of the meerkat acts as insulation and a cooling system to keep heat in when needed and to cool its body when needed. All meerkats in a gang work to provide for and protect the members of their gang.

FEATURES
- The meerkat is a member of the mongoose family and is recognized for its long, thin body.
- It has markings on its back and darker bands around the eyes. It also has black-tipped ears and tail. The color of its fur ranges from silver to orange to brown.

FUN FACTS
- Meerkats live in groups called gangs or mobs.
- One meerkat stands guard while the others in the mob play, hunt, or sleep.
- An adult meerkat will protect its young from predators and will even sacrifice its life for its young's life.

CREATED KIND MEMBERS
Mongoose

CLASS:	Mammalia (mammal)
ORDER:	Carnivora (meat-eating)
FAMILY:	Herpestidae (mongoose)
GENUS/SPECIES:	*Suricata suricatta*
Size:	Average about 20 in long (0.5 m)
Weight:	Average about 1.5 lbs (0.7 kg)
Original Diet:	Plants
Present Diet:	Mainly insects; but also plants and small vertebrates
Habitat:	Savannas of southern Africa

MOLE

MOLE
CREATED ON DAY 6

DESIGN

The claws of the mole are specifically designed to tear through and remove dirt. The mole breaks up the dirt and then push it behind itself. Frequently the mole will turn around and push the dirt to the surface. The tiny eyes of the mole are covered by a thin layer of skin that protects them from dirt, and its nose is used for pushing up insects and dirt.

FEATURES

- The mole is an interesting creature with large, spade-like front paws and a round body.
- The mole has no neck separating its head from its body.

FUN FACTS

- The mole uses its sensitive nose to detect movement, temperature changes, and other moles since it has poor eyesight and hearing.
- The mole's fur moves both forward and backward. This keeps the dirt from getting caught next to its skin.

CREATED KIND MEMBERS

Shrew mole, Russian desman

CLASS:	Mammalia (mammal)
ORDER:	Insectivora (insect-eating)
FAMILY:	Talpidae (moles)
GENUS/SPECIES:	42 species make up the Talpidae family
Size:	About 6 in long (0.2 m)
Weight:	Between 2 and 4 oz (0.1 kg)
Original Diet:	Plants
Present Diet:	Mostly insects
Habitat:	Forests and fields

MOOSE

MOOSE
CREATED ON DAY 6

DESIGN

God designed the moose with powerful front and hind feet to protect it from predators. An unwary predator can be killed by these powerful defenses. These defenses were not necessary until after the Fall, since animals did not eat other animals before then.

FEATURES

- The moose is the largest member of the deer family and is known for its tremendous antlers, which occur only on the bulls.
- The moose has long, dark hair that provides needed insulation from the cold. Its nose is long and flexible.

FUN FACTS

- The bull moose sheds and regrows its antlers every year.
- A moose's hair is hollow.
- The moose can rotate its ears 180° which allows it to locate predators from great distances.
- The largest subspecies of the moose is found in Alaska.
- Newborn calves weigh 28–35 lbs (13–16 kg), and within five months they can grow to over 300 lbs (136 kg).

CREATED KIND MEMBERS

Deer, reindeer, elk

CLASS:	Mammalia (mammal)
ORDER:	Artiodactyla (even-toed hooves)
FAMILY:	Cervidae (deer kind)
GENUS/SPECIES:	*Alces alces*
Size:	7–10 ft (2–3 m)
Weight:	Average of 1,300 lbs (590 kg)
Original Diet:	Plants
Present Diet:	Plants
Habitat:	Northern forests of Europe, Russia, and North America

NORTH AMERICAN ELK

NORTH AMERICAN ELK
CREATED ON DAY 6

DESIGN

When a buck grows new antlers for the year, these antlers are very sensitive and somewhat soft. However, they are protected by a layer of skin called "velvet" that the buck removes just before mating season begins by rubbing his antlers on trees. How did the elk know to rub this layer of skin from his antlers? This instinct was given to the elk by its Creator God.

FEATURES

- The North American elk is usually a shade of brown with darker shading on its neck, belly, head, and legs.
- It also has a dark, shaggy mane hanging from its neck to its chest.

FUN FACTS

- The number of tines on the elk's antlers does not necessarily give the age of the elk because some bucks have antlers that are uneven (three on one side and four on the other). Also, the number of tines can actually decrease with age.
- This species also occurs in Siberia. It is the second largest species of deer in the world.
- Male elk are called bulls and females are called cows.
- This species is often called "wapiti," which is a Shawnee word meaning "white rump."

CREATED KIND MEMBERS

Deer, reindeer, moose

CLASS:	Mammalia (mammals)
ORDER:	Artiodactyla (even-toed hooves)
FAMILY:	Cervidae (deer kind)
GENUS/SPECIES:	*Cervus canadensis*
Size:	5–9 ft (1.6–2.7 m) tall
Weight:	375–1,100 lbs (170–500 kg)
Original Diet:	Plants
Present Diet:	Plants
Habitat:	Grasslands and open forests of North America and Siberia

NORTH AMERICAN PORCUPINE

NORTH AMERICAN PORCUPINE
CREATED ON DAY 6

DESIGN

The porcupine does not throw its quills, but it uses its strong tail to push its quills into an attacker. However, a porcupine's quills were not used as defensive weapons until after the Fall. The limbs of the porcupine are designed for climbing and feeding in trees. The pads on its feet are textured to grab the tree surface, and it uses its quills as hooks that prevent the porcupine from sliding backward while it is feeding with its front feet.

FEATURES

- The porcupine is most known for the thousands of quills that cover its body. All but the snout, belly, throat, and feet pads are covered with these barbed quills.

FUN FACTS

- The porcupine lives in trees if dens are unavailable, and it is primarily nocturnal.
- It likes salt.
- The porcupine is a good swimmer.

CREATED KIND MEMBERS

Hairy dwarf porcupine, Brazilian porcupine

CLASS:	Mammalia (mammal)
ORDER:	Rodentia (rodents)
FAMILY:	Erethizontidae (New World porcupines)
GENUS/SPECIES:	*Erethizon dorsatum*
Size:	3–4 ft (1–1.2 m)
Weight:	10–40 lbs (4.5–18 kg); normally between 7–15 lbs (3–7 kg)
Original Diet:	Plants
Present Diet:	Bark of trees and plants
Habitat:	Timbered areas in Alaska, Canada, the United States, and northern Mexico

OKAPI

OKAPI
CREATED ON DAY 6

DESIGN

The unusual appearance of the okapi provides this animal with excellent camouflage in the forests when sunlight filters in through the trees. The okapi is part of the giraffe kind; it is not a link between zebras and giraffes, as some scientists claim. If the okapi had a long neck like its relative the giraffe, it would have a difficult time moving through the thick forests.

FEATURES

- The okapi is unusual since its front and hind legs resemble the zebra while other features resemble the giraffe.
- The male okapi has small, hair-covered horns.

FUN FACTS

- The okapi's tongue is long enough to clean out its eyes and ears.
- Its fur is very oily, keeping the animal dry on rainy days.
- The okapi wasn't known to the scientific world until around 1900, but Pygmies who share their forest home with the okapis have killed and eaten them for centuries.
- The okapi is native just to the Ituri forest of the northeastern part of the Democratic Republic of Congo.

CREATED KIND MEMBERS

Giraffe

CLASS: Mammalia (mammal)
ORDER: Artiodactyla (even-toed hooves)
FAMILY: Giraffidae (giraffe kind)
GENUS/SPECIES: *Okapi johnstoni*

Size: About 5 ft (1.5 m)
Weight: 440–770 lbs (200–300 kg); Females are larger than the males
Original Diet: Plants
Present Diet: Plants
Habitat: Eastern equatorial rainforest of Africa

POLAR BEAR

POLAR BEAR
CREATED ON DAY 6

DESIGN

The polar bear is a smart hunter. It will spend hours beside the breathing hole of a seal in the ice. When the seal emerges for air, the polar bear will use its claws to grab the seal. This instinct came into play after the Fall. The paws of the polar bear are uniquely adapted for its life on snow and ice. The fur helps it grip the ice, and the partial webbing between the toes aids in swimming.

FEATURES

- The polar bears is known for what appears to be its pure white fur and massive size. It is the largest of the bear kind.

FUN FACTS

- The polar bear's skin is actually black. This helps absorb heat from the sun.
- The fur is made of clear, hollow tubes, and it covers even the bottoms of its paws.
- The polar bear is often found far from land on drifting ice floes.
- It is equally comfortable in the water and on land and it can travel up to 5,500 miles (8,860 km) a year.
- The distribution of the polar bear roughly follows the southernmost limit of ice floes.

CREATED KIND MEMBERS

Brown bear, panda, black bear

CLASS:	Mammalia (mammal)
ORDER:	Carnivora (meat-eating)
FAMILY:	Ursidae (bear kind)
GENUS/SPECIES:	*Ursus maritimus*
Size:	8–11 ft (2.4–3.4 m)
Weight:	500–1,500 lbs (250–680 kg); Males are larger than females
Original Diet:	Plants
Present Diet:	Mostly seals; also fish, plants, and birds
Habitat:	Tundra and sea ice in Arctic regions of the Northern Hemisphere

PRAIRIE DOG

PRAIRIE DOG
CREATED ON DAY 6

DESIGN

Prairie dogs live together in large groups called towns. These towns are made up of separate territories that are dominated by one male. This organization provides safety from predators since "watchdogs" are on the lookout for predators. Without this organization the prairie dog would be susceptible to danger. This instinct was not needed until after the Fall, when animals began hunting other animals.

FEATURES

- The different species of prairie dog vary in color from red and yellow to brown and black. Most have pale patches of fur and colored tails.
- Prairie dogs eat grass and keep it cropped short so they can have an unobstructed view of any approaching predators.

FUN FACTS

- The largest prairie dog town had a population of over 400 million.
- Prairie dogs exhibit behaviors that we would call unselfish. Since they live in territories with many individual members, they share their food supply and burrows, which can make for skimpy meals and tight quarters.

CREATED KIND MEMBERS

Ground squirrel, chipmunk

CLASS:	Mammalia (mammal)
ORDER:	Rodentia (rodents)
FAMILY:	Sciuridae (squirrels)
GENUS/SPECIES:	5 species within the sub-family Cynomys
Size:	10–13 in (0.3 m)
Weight:	1–3 lbs (0.5–1.4 kg)
Original Diet:	Plants
Present Diet:	Plants and sometimes insects
Habitat:	Open plains and plateaus from North Dakota to a small area in northern Mexico

RABBIT

RABBIT
CREATED ON DAY 6

DESIGN

Even secular biologists claim that rabbits are hardly different from the earliest rabbit fossils. This is because rabbits were created only thousands of years ago with only slight variations occurring within their kind since creation. The eyes of the rabbit are placed in the perfect spot to allow them to see almost in a complete circle. Some species have broader feet—a special design feature that allows them to run efficiently on snow.

FEATURES

- In general, hares are larger than rabbits although they both have many of the same features. Another difference is that hares have longer and black-tipped ears.
- Different species are colored from white to dark brown.
- Female rabbits are usually larger than males.

FUN FACTS

- The Romans were the first to domesticate the rabbit, and the rabbit spread as the Roman Empire spread.
- Some species use their feet to communicate to others by pounding their hind legs on the ground.
- The introduction of rabbits to Australia from Europe has contributed to the extinction of many native plants and animals.

CREATED KIND MEMBERS

Jackrabbit, snowshoe hare

CLASS:	Mammalia (mammal)
ORDER:	Lagomorpha (gnawing, herbivorous mammals)
FAMILY:	Leporidae (hares and rabbits)
GENUS/SPECIES:	Over 54 species
Size:	Between 1 and 2 ft long (0.3–0.6 m)
Weight:	0.5 lb–15 lbs (0.3–7 kg)
Original Diet:	Plants
Present Diet:	Grasses
Habitat:	Grasslands and forests worldwide except for Antarctica, Madagascar, and parts of the Middle East

REINDEER

REINDEER
CREATED ON DAY 6

DESIGN

A reindeer is known to paw at the snow to uncover its food, even when two or three feet (0.6–0.9 m) cover the plants. How does the reindeer know to do this? God designed it this way. The reindeer's coat is made of dense, short hair that is hollow, enabling it to hold air and shed water, making it perfect for the colder temperatures where the reindeer lives.

FEATURES

- Most reindeer are brown with a gray underbelly, which helps them blend into the snow during winter. Their antlers are reddish or grayish brown.
- Caribou and reindeer are the same species, reindeer being a domesticated, smaller variety or caribou and classified scientifically as a subspecies.

FUN FACTS

- Reindeer and caribou are the only deer with fur on their nose pads.
- These domesticated caribou are prized for their milk, meat, and leather.
- The main food of reindeer is lichen, but they will also eat grasses along with twigs and mushrooms.

CREATED KIND MEMBERS

Deer, elk, moose

CLASS:	Mammalia (mammal)
ORDER:	Artiodactyla (even-toed hooves)
FAMILY:	Cervidae (deer kind)
GENUS/SPECIES:	*Rangifer tarandus* (9 subspecies)
Size:	Vary from 3–8 ft (0.9–2.5 m), not including the antlers
Weight:	120–700 lbs (54–318 kg)
Original Diet:	Plants
Present Diet:	Plants
Habitat:	Most occur in Scandinavia and Siberia

RHINOCEROS

RHINOCEROS
CREATED ON DAY 6

DESIGN

Rhinos are herbivores, meaning that they eat only plants. White rhinos (indigenous to Africa) are uniquely suited to graze on grass with their square-shaped lips. The other four species of rhinos prefer to eat the foliage of trees or bushes.

FEATURES

- The rhino is known for its immense body and stubby legs. Rhinos have either one or two horns on its heads, which are used in fighting with other rhinos and for protection against predators.
- These are some of the most endangered animals in the world. They continue to be fiercely hunted for their horns.

FUN FACTS

- A rhino can sleep while lying down or while standing up.
- Rhinos may have been the source for the legendary unicorn.
- A rhino's skin gives the appearance of bony plates, but it is really just thick and wrinkled skin.
- The gestation period for a baby rhino (calf) is 14–18 months, depending on the species.

CREATED KIND MEMBERS

White rhinoceros, woolly rhinoceros (extinct)

CLASS:	Mammalia (mammal)
ORDER:	Perissodactyla (nonruminant mammals with odd-numbered toes)
FAMILY:	Rhinocerotidae (rhinoceros)
GENUS/SPECIES:	5 different species (2 African and 3 Asian)
Size:	4–6 ft tall (1.5–1.8 m)
Weight:	750–8,000 lbs (340–3,600 kg), depending on species
Original Diet:	Plants
Present Diet:	Plants
Habitat:	Savannas and forests of tropical and subtropical Africa and Asia

SEA OTTER

SEA OTTER
CREATED ON DAY 6

DESIGN

The sea otter is one of the few animals known to use tools. It uses small rocks or other objects to pry prey from rocks and to hammer or pry open its food. An otter can dive up to 330 ft (100 m) when foraging for food. God gave the sea otter the thickest fur in the animal kingdom. Unlike other marine mammals, the sea otter does not have a layer of blubber (fat) to help keep it warm.

FEATURES

- The ears and nostrils close when the otter is underwater.
- The sea otter has webbed hind feet which are perfect for swimming; its forefeet are smaller with semi-retractable claws.

FUN FACTS

- A sea otter's fur has an estimated 650,000 hairs per square inch.
- Since the sea otter must produce a large amount of heat on its own, it must eat about 20 lbs (9 kg) of food a day.
- The sea otter sleeps and rests on its back, usually anchored in a kelp (seaweed) bed.

CREATED KIND MEMBERS

Weasel, badger, wolverine, ferret

CLASS:	Mammalia (mammal)
ORDER:	Carnivora (meat-eating)
FAMILY:	Mustelidae (sub-family Lutrinae)
GENUS/SPECIES:	*Enhydra lutris*
Size:	4–5 ft (1.2–1.5 m)
Weight:	Average between 64 and 85 lbs (29–39 kg)
Original Diet:	Plants
Present Diet:	Mostly sea creatures including clams, crabs, fish, and octopus
Habitat:	Pacific coastal and estuarine areas of North America

SLOTH

SLOTH
CREATED ON DAY 6

DESIGN
Both species of sloth have long forearms and strong hind limbs. These features are perfectly designed for climbing and living in trees. Much of the sloth's fur is covered by a type of algae. This algae helps camouflage the animal while it is in the trees.

FEATURES
- Sloths vary in color from gray and tan to dark brown. They have long, shaggy fur that points to the ground when the sloth is hanging upside down. This allows rain water to be easily shed from their fur, keeping them dry. Some sloths even have thicker hair around the neck, which forms a mane.
- The hair of sloths grows in the opposite direction of most other mammals: from the stomach to the back.

FUN FACTS
- Sloths spend most of theirs lives hanging upside down in trees. They eat, sleep, and give birth while upside down.
- Sloths get their name from their extremely slow movements while on the ground and in trees.

CREATED KIND MEMBERS
Three-toed sloth, ground sloth

CLASS:	Mammalia (mammal)
ORDER:	Xenarthra (strange-jointed)
FAMILY:	Megalonychidae and Bradypodidae (three-toed and two-toed)
GENUS/SPECIES:	5 different species within the two families—*Bradypus* and *Choloepus*
Size:	Both genera about 1.6 ft (0.5 m)
Weight:	*Bradypus*: 6.5–11 lbs (3–5 kg); *Choloepus*: 20 lbs (9 kg)
Original Diet:	Plants
Present Diet:	Plants
Habitat:	Forests of Central and South America

SPOTTED HYENA

SPOTTED HYENA
CREATED ON DAY 6

DESIGN

Some consider the hyena to be the link between cats and dogs. But this is not true since the cat and the dog are two separate kinds of animals; there is no transition between them. Spotted hyenas hunt their prey in groups of two to five; this allows them to bring down a larger animal. This hunting instinct was not part of their behavior until after the Fall, since all animals were originally created to eat plants.

FEATURES

- The spotted hyena is often tan or reddish brown with dark brown or black spots over its body. It has a black nose and tail. The spots of the older hyenas are drastically faded, compared to the darker spots of the young.
- The spotted hyena is nocturnal and lives in holes in the ground, in caves, or in lairs in dense vegetation.

FUN FACTS

- The spotted hyena can digest bone, horn, and teeth.
- This animal is also known as the laughing hyena for the call it makes.
- The lifespan of the spotted hyena is about 25 years.
- The female weighs more than the male.

CREATED KIND MEMBERS

Brown hyena, striped hyena

CLASS:	Mammalia (mammal)
ORDER:	Carnivora (meat-eating)
FAMILY:	Hyaenidae (hyenas)
GENUS/SPECIES:	*Crocuta crocuta*
Size:	Average about 3 ft (0.9 m) tall; 3–5 ft (0.9–1.5 m) long
Weight:	From 120–165 lbs (55–75 kg)
Original Diet:	Plants
Present Diet:	Wildebeest, zebra, gazelle, and wild buffalo, some carrion, and large numbers of locusts
Habitat:	Mostly savannas and forests of sub-Saharan Africa

STRIPED SKUNK

STRIPED SKUNK
CREATED ON DAY 6

DESIGN

Originally the skunk kind did not use its musk to protect itself from its enemies because it had no enemies. Skunks are mostly nocturnal animals. This feature keeps skunks and humans from accidental contact during the day. However, if contact does occur, the skunk will give fair warning before detonating its weapon. A unique feature of the skunk is its ability to delay the implantation of a fertilized egg. This allows the skunk to give birth in the spring when chances of survival for the young are the best.

FEATURES

- The striped skunk is readily identified by its black body and two white stripes along its back and tail. The stripe length and width vary with each individual.
- Its claws are longer on the front feet to aid in digging.

FUN FACTS

- The striped skunk is the most common one in North America.
- The fluid of the skunk, from the two glands near the base of the tail, has been used as a basis for many perfumes.
- The striped skunk may also eat trash that is left out by humans.
- A skunk can spray up to 10–20 ft (3–6 m).

CREATED KIND MEMBERS

Western spotted skunk, hooded skunk, hog-nosed skunk

CLASS:	Mammalia (mammal)
ORDER:	Carnivora (meat-eating)
FAMILY:	Mephitidae (skunks and stinker badgers)
GENUS/SPECIES:	*Mephitis mephitis*
Size:	21–27 in (0.5–0.7 m); tail is 9–13 in (0.2–0.3 m)
Weight:	2.5–10 lbs (1.1–4.5 kg)
Original Diet:	Plants
Present Diet:	Insects, small mammals, fish, and carrion
Habitat:	Forests, plains, and deserts, as well as urban areas

TASMANIAN DEVIL

TASMANIAN DEVIL
CREATED ON DAY 6

DESIGN

The Tasmanian devil is the scavenger of the forest, eating left-over carcasses and other dead animals. Without it, diseases would be more rampant in the forest, placing other animals in danger. The Tasmanian devil has strong, heavy molars and powerful jaws that tear and crush its food, which can include the bone and fur of dead animals. However, these powerful teeth were originally used to eat plants.

FEATURES

- This small marsupial is covered with short, black fur with white markings on its throat. White patches may also be seen on its side and rump.
- The Tasmanian devil is energetic and curious, and it travels long distances each night looking for its food.

FUN FACTS

- During a fight, the ears of a Tasmanian devil can turn red.
- When under stress, the Tasmanian devil can release a strong, foul odor.
- When a group of Tasmanian devils feeds together at a carcass, harsh screeching and spine-chilling screams can be heard.

CREATED KIND MEMBERS

Mulgara, kowari, northern quoll

CLASS:	Mammalia (mammal)
ORDER:	Dasyuromorphia (dasyuroid marsupials and marsupial carnivores)
FAMILY:	Dasyuridae
GENUS/SPECIES:	*Sarcophilus laniarius*
Size:	23–26 in (0.6–0.7 m)
Weight:	13–18 lbs (6–8 kg)
Original Diet:	Plants
Present Diet:	Carrion
Habitat:	Forests of Tasmania, in dense underbrush

WALLABY

WALLABY
CREATED ON DAY 6

DESIGN

If the wallaby didn't have such a long, thick tail, it would probably fall over on its nose. The tail is the perfect balance for the animal. For the young to survive after birth, it must make its way into the pouch where it will remain until it is fully developed. The young does not emerge from its mother's pouch until it is about 5 months old. The female's pouch is specifically designed to aid the joey in development and survival.

FEATURES

- These creatures are smaller than kangaroos but similar in appearance.
- Their coloring can vary from dark shades of brown to yellow or tan.
- Some species, called rock-wallabies, occur in rugged terrain and have modified feet designed to grip rock effectively, similar to goats of the northern hemisphere.

FUN FACTS

- Some species lick their hands to cool themselves when the weather is hot or when they are excited.
- Some brush-tailed rock-wallabies escaped from a zoo on Oahu in Hawaii in 1916 and established a feral population in Kalihi Valley, which exists to this day.

CREATED KIND MEMBERS

Kangaroo

CLASS:	Mammalia (mammals)
ORDER:	Diprotodontia (kangaroos, possums, wallabies, and relatives)
FAMILY:	Macropodidae (kangaroos, wallabies, and relatives)
GENUS/SPECIES:	3 subspecies
Size:	Varies greatly within species; 2–6 ft (0.6–2 m) tall
Weight:	Varies greatly within species; 12–50 lbs (6–25 kg)
Original Diet:	Plants
Present Diet:	Grasses and other plants
Habitat:	Forests and savannas of Australia

WALRUS

WALRUS
CREATED ON DAY 6

DESIGN

The thick, wrinkled skin of the walrus acts as a protective barrier when it fights with other walruses and when it is attacked by predators. The walrus also has a thick layer of blubber under its skin that protects it from the freezing water. When the temperature drops, the walrus' blood vessels get smaller. This helps it deal with the changing temperatures in its habitat.

FEATURES

- The walrus is known for its large size and pink–reddish brown coloring.
- It is also easily recognized by its large tusks.

FUN FACTS

- The tusks of the walrus have growth rings just like a tree, and are used to protect it from attacks by polar bears and killer whales.
- The walrus uses its whiskers to find its invertebrate food, sometimes diving down 300 ft (91 m) to retrieve its very favorite food, clams, from the ocean floor.
- Air sacs in the walrus' neck allow it to sleep with its head held up in the water.
- Commercial hunting, mainly for the ivory in its tusks, depleted the numbers of walrus, but it has been federally protected in the U.S. since 1972.

CREATED KIND MEMBERS

Pacific walrus

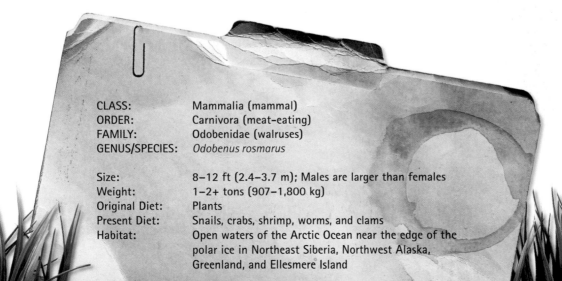

CLASS:	Mammalia (mammal)
ORDER:	Carnivora (meat-eating)
FAMILY:	Odobenidae (walruses)
GENUS/SPECIES:	*Odobenus rosmarus*
Size:	8–12 ft (2.4–3.7 m); Males are larger than females
Weight:	1–2+ tons (907–1,800 kg)
Original Diet:	Plants
Present Diet:	Snails, crabs, shrimp, worms, and clams
Habitat:	Open waters of the Arctic Ocean near the edge of the polar ice in Northeast Siberia, Northwest Alaska, Greenland, and Ellesmere Island

WARTHOG

WARTHOG
CREATED ON DAY 6

DESIGN

The warts on this animal actually protects its face during attack. Since it does not have a layer of fat under its skin, the warthog is susceptible to drastic temperature changes. To escape these extremes, it wallows in mud to cool down, or it enters its burrow and huddles with others to keep warm.

FEATURES

- The warthog looks very similar to a pig or a hog, but it is known for its warty face and large, protruding tusks.
- Warthogs are usually black or brown.

FUN FACTS

- The warthog lets birds perch on it and eat parasites that are on its body. This helps to keep the warthog healthy.
- After a night's sleep, a warthog will dash out of its burrow to get a head-start on any predator that may be lurking nearby.

CREATED KIND MEMBERS

Red river hog, bush pig

CLASS:	Mammalia (mammal)
ORDER:	Artiodactyla (even–toed hooves)
FAMILY:	Suidae (hog kind)
GENUS/SPECIES:	*Phacochoerus africanus* and *P. aethiopicus* (common and desert warthogs)
Size:	2–5 ft long (0.9–1.5 m); 2 ft tall (0.6 m)
Weight:	110–330 lbs (50–150 kg)
Original Diet:	Plants
Present Diet:	Grass, roots, bark, berries, sometimes carrion
Habitat:	Savannas and forests of Africa

WILDEBEEST

WILDEBEEST
CREATED ON DAY 6

DESIGN

Less than an hour after birth, a young wildebeest can keep up with the herd. This ability was designed by its Creator to increase its chance for survival. Traveling in large packs makes the wildebeest safer from predators. If a predator enters the pack while it is running, the predator is in danger of being killed by the herd itself. Also when traveling, wildebeest sleep in rows. This gives them protection, as well as a quick escape in case of danger in the night.

FEATURES

- The wildebeest is known for its pronounced muzzle and horns.
- It normally has longer, darker hair on its back and a black face, tail, and mane.
- Wildebeest are also known as gnus.

FUN FACTS

- Wildebeest migrate each year to find fresh pastures. These migrating herds can contain up to onc million individuals, and they sometimes include zebras and gazelles as well.

CREATED KIND MEMBERS

Yak, antelope, gazelle

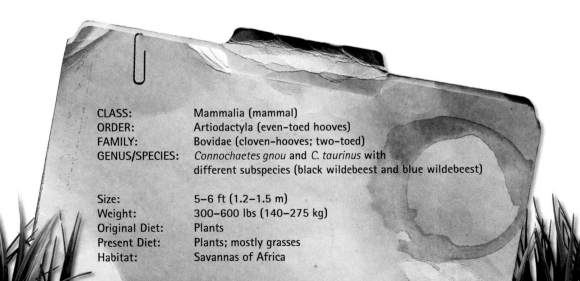

CLASS:	Mammalia (mammal)
ORDER:	Artiodactyla (even-toed hooves)
FAMILY:	Bovidae (cloven-hooves; two-toed)
GENUS/SPECIES:	*Connochaetes gnou* and *C. taurinus* with different subspecies (black wildebeest and blue wildebeest)
Size:	5–6 ft (1.2–1.5 m)
Weight:	300–600 lbs (140–275 kg)
Original Diet:	Plants
Present Diet:	Plants; mostly grasses
Habitat:	Savannas of Africa

WOLVERINE

WOLVERINE
CREATED ON DAY 6

DESIGN

The wolverine is specifically designed for cold, snowy habitats. The wolverine is also designed with great strength, sharp claws, and fearlessness. If this animal were large, like a bear, it would be the strongest animal on earth. The wolverine's aggression to other animals developed after the Fall; it was not part of its original nature.

FEATURES

- With its long, dense, black fur and white stripes, the wolverine is sometimes referred to as the skunk bear, even though it is not a bear or a skunk.
- Females are smaller and lighter than males.

FUN FACTS

- Larger animals, like the cougar, will back down from fighting a wolverine.
- No animal hunts the wolverine. Humans are its only enemy.
- The wolverine is usually terrestrial, but it can climb trees with considerable speed.

CREATED KIND MEMBERS

Weasel, otter, badger, ferret

CLASS:	Mammalia (mammal)
ORDER:	Carnivora (meat-eating)
FAMILY:	Mustelidae (badgers, otters, and relatives)
GENUS/SPECIES:	*Gulo gulo*
Size:	36–45 in long (0.9–1.2 m)
Weight:	25–36 lbs (11–16 kg)
Original Diet:	Plants
Present Diet:	Rodents, large mammals, carrion, eggs of ground-nesting birds
Habitat:	Arctic regions, in taiga and tundra

WOMBAT

WOMBAT
CREATED ON DAY 6

DESIGN

The female wombat has a pouch that opens toward the rear. This design is important since the wombat digs its tunnels underground. If the pouch opened toward the front, it would possibly fill with dirt as it dug its tunnel. The wombat is designed with powerful legs and extremely strong claws, which it uses for efficient digging and feeding.

FEATURES

- This marsupial is a stocky animals with powerful front paws and short, dark fur. The fur's shade and texture depends on the species.
- The wombat resembles a small bear in general appearance.

FUN FACTS

- A wombat can run about 25 mph (40 km/h).
- Wombats build different sizes of tunnels for different uses. Smaller tunnels are dug for quick escape while longer, larger tunnels are used for sleeping and mating.
- The wombat is a shy and timid creature; and, therefore, it is difficult to observe in the wild.

CREATED KIND MEMBERS

Common wombat, hairy-nosed wombat

CLASS:	Mammalia (mammal)
ORDER:	Diprotodontia (kangaroos, possums, and relatives)
FAMILY:	Vombatidae (wombats)
GENUS/SPECIES:	*Vombatus ursinus, Lasiorhinus latrifrons*, and *L. krefftii* (coarse-haired, northern hairy-nosed, and southern hairy-nosed)
Size:	Average: 3.3 ft (1 m)
Weight:	33–88 lbs (15–40 kg)
Original Diet:	Plants
Present Diet:	Grasses
Habitat:	Savannas and forests of Australia, Tasmania, and Flinders Island

YAK

YAK
CREATED ON DAY 6

DESIGN

The yak is designed with large lungs, a high red-blood cell count, and a high concentration of blood sugar. These features enable the yak able to survive in higher elevations. Many mountain-dwelling humans use the yak as a beast of burden since it can survive in such a demanding habitat.

FEATURES

- The yak has blackish brown hair that covers the entire body and tail. It also has large, curving horns.
- The domesticated yak is considerably smaller and more varied in color than its wild relatives.

FUN FACTS

- Despite its large size, a yak would rather run from a fight. However, it will charge if it feels sufficiently threatened.
- The yak has been domesticated for its fur, strength, and milk.
- The yak can live at elevations as high as 20,000 ft (6,100 m).

CREATED KIND MEMBERS

Antelope, wildebeest, gazelle

CLASS:	Mammalia (mammals)
ORDER:	Artiodactyla (even-toed hooves)
FAMILY:	Bovidae (antelope, cattle, gazelle, sheep, goats, and relatives)
GENUS/SPECIES:	*Bos grunniens*
Size:	Average: 6.5 ft (2 m)
Weight:	Average: 1,430 lbs (650 kg)
Original Diet:	Plants
Present Diet:	Plants
Habitat:	High mountain tundra of Asia

ZEBRA

ZEBRA
CREATED ON DAY 6

DESIGN

The stripes of a zebra are designed to give it protection from predators. When they are running in a pack, it is difficult for the predator to pick out just one since their stripes seem to blend together. This design became very helpful after the Fall when some animals became predators of them. A zebra eats grass and other plants, which wears down its teeth; however, its teeth never stop growing, so its ability to eat is not hindered.

FEATURES

- Each species of zebra has its own unique striping pattern in its size, color, and placement.

FUN FACTS

- At night while the herd sleeps, one zebra stays awake on lookout. This responsibility is shared.
- Zebras smile. Their grimace is used to greet other zebras.
- The zebra has excellent hearing and eyesight and can run at speeds up to 35 mph (56 km/h).
- A question frequently debated is whether zebras are white with black stripes or black with white stripes. What do you think?

CREATED KIND MEMBERS

Thoroughbred and Arabian horses, Shetland pony

CLASS:	Mammalia (mammal)
ORDER:	Perissodactyla (odd-toed hooves)
FAMILY:	Equidae (horse kind)
GENUS/SPECIES:	*Equus grevyi*, *Equus zebra*, and *Equus burchelli* (Grevy's, mountain, and Burchell's)
Size:	Around 4 ft (1.2 m) at the shoulder
Weight:	550–900 lbs (250–430 kg)
Original Diet:	Plants
Present Diet:	Grasses
Habitat:	Plains, savannas, and some mountainous regions of Africa

ANDEAN CONDOR

ANDEAN CONDOR
CREATED ON DAY 5

DESIGN

The condor helps keep the environment clean from potentially harmful bacteria found on animal carcasses. God designed within them the ability to eat much of what other animals will not eat, but this feature did not become part of their habit until after the Fall. The condor will ride air currents, similar to the eagle. This is an efficient way of flying for a bird of its size.

FEATURES

- The condor has weak feet that are used more for walking than clutching food.
- Feathers are absent from most of its head and neck.

FUN FACTS

- The Andean condor can be considered one of nature's garbage collectors.
- It can pick an animal's carcass clean in under an hour—sometimes even eating the bones.
- The Andean condor nests in shallow caves on cliff ledges and lays a single egg.

CREATED KIND MEMBERS

California condor, turkey vulture

CLASS:	Aves (birds)
ORDER:	Ciconiiformes (storks and relatives)
FAMILY:	Cathartidae (New World vultures)
GENUS/SPECIES:	*Vultur gryphus*
Size:	Body: 40–50 in (1–1.3 m); Wingspan: 10–12 ft (3.2–3.7 m)
Weight:	Males: 24–33 lbs (11–15 kg); Females: 18–23 lbs (8.2–10.4 kg)
Original Diet:	Plants
Present Diet:	Primarily carrion, but also eggs from seabird colonies
Habitat:	Andes, from Venezuela to Sierra del Fuego; descends to lowland desert regions in Peru and Chile

BALD EAGLE

BALD EAGLE
CREATED ON DAY 5

DESIGN

The eyesight of the bald eagle is 6 to 8 times better than a human's. This excellent vision allows it to sight its prey while high in the air. The talons of the eagle are used to grasp its prey while in flight. An eagle in flight uses the air currents to give it momentum and lift. How does it know how to do this, except its kind was designed with this knowledge at its creation.

FEATURES

- The term bald eagle comes from the word "balde," which in Old English means "white." This species is known for its white head and tail and its dark brown body.

FUN FACTS

- The bald eagle became the national bird of the United States in 1782.
- The head of a young bald eagle is actually brown until the eagle matures, which takes 4–5 years.
- A bald eagle's nest can weigh up to 2 tons (2,030 kg)! Pairs of this species often return to the same next year after year and add material to it.

CREATED KIND MEMBERS

Osprey, sea eagle, Madagascar fish eagle

CLASS:	Aves (birds)
ORDER:	Falconiformes (diurnal birds of prey)
FAMILY:	Accipitridae (hawks, eagles, Old World vultures)
GENUS/SPECIES:	*Haliaeetus leucocephalus*
Size:	Wingspan up to 8 ft (2.3 m)
Weight:	Female: 10–14 lbs (4.5–6.3 kg), Male: 8–10 lbs (3.6–4.5 kg)
Original Diet:	Plants
Present Diet:	Fish, small mammals, and aquatic birds
Habitat:	Alaska, Canada, and the continental United States, on sea coasts or near rivers and lakes

COCKATIEL

COCKATIEL
CREATED ON DAY 5

DESIGN
The cockatiel has a sharply bent beak, which is perfectly designed for eating seeds and berries. Millions of alleged mutations cannot explain this design feature.

FEATURES
- The male is the more brightly colored with its yellow face, forehead, throat, and crest while its tail is gray.
- The female is duller with yellow laterals in the otherwise gray tail.
- Both sexes have orange cheek patches and white patches on their wings.

FUN FACTS
- The cockatiel enters its nest hole backward (tail-first).
- The male and female take turns incubating the eggs.
- A cockatiel can learn to mimic sounds such as a car alarm, a ringing telephone, or calls of other birds.
- Cockatiels are strongly nomadic, moving in search of food and water.

CREATED KIND MEMBERS
Cockatoo, corella

CLASS:	Aves (birds)
ORDER:	Psittaciformes (parrots)
FAMILY:	Cacatuidae (cockatoo)
GENUS/SPECIES:	*Nymphicus hollandicus*
Size:	Up to 13 in (0.3 m)
Weight:	3–3.5 oz (85–100g)
Original Diet:	Plants
Present Diet:	Grains, seeds, fruits, nuts, and berries
Habitat:	Australia and Tasmania in open country

DEMOISELLE CRANE

DEMOISELLE CRANE
CREATED ON DAY 5

DESIGN
Two unique features of this crane are its toes, which are shorter than the toes of other cranes, and its bill, which is also shorter than the bills of other cranes. These are designs given this species to adapt to its habitat. The short toes allow it to run on the hard, dry ground while its short bill allows it to better find food in its habitat.

FEATURES
- The demoiselle crane, whether male or female, sports an array of gray, white, and black feathers. It has red eyes and a multi-colored beak, from olive green to orange.
- The demoiselle is the smallest crane, the male being slightly larger than the female.

FUN FACTS
- This bird like many others will pretend to be injured in order to lure predators away from its nest.
- To attract a mate, the demoiselle crane will partake in an elaborate courtship dance that involves leaping, calling, bowing, and head-bobbing.

CREATED KIND MEMBERS
Common crane, sandhill crane

CLASS: Aves (birds)
ORDER: Gruiformes (coots, cranes and rails)
FAMILY: Gruidae (cranes)
GENUS/SPECIES: *Ardea virgo*

Size: 3 ft (0.9 m)
Weight: Between 4 and 6 lbs (2–2.7 kg)
Original Diet: Plants
Present Diet: Mainly seeds, grass, and other plant material; insects, and even lizards
Habitat: Savannas in higher elevations near water, in central Eurasia; winters in India and sub-Saharan Africa

EMPEROR PENGUIN

EMPEROR PENGUIN
CREATED ON DAY 5

DESIGN

Baby penguins hatch at just the right time. During the winter months when the young hatch, the ocean is farthest away from the penguins. By the time the young are ready to enter the ocean, the ice pack has melted, bringing the water's edge closest to them. To keep warm against the harsh Antarctic wind and subzero temperatures while incubating the egg, the male emperor penguin huddles with other males in a huge circle. They take turns moving from the outer, colder area to the inner, warmer area. This instinct is part of God's protection for this species.

FEATURES

- The emperor penguin is the largest of the penguin species.
- An orange-yellow band extends from behind the eyes of this penguin downward to the neck and chest area. There is also orange coloring on its lower beak.
- The emperor penguin is easily recognized with its jet black head, grayish-black wings and back, and white belly.
- All penguins are flightless on land, but do "fly" very well under water.

FUN FACTS

- The male incubates the egg during the harsh Antarctic winter. He carries it on his feet and protects it in his brood pouch while the female leaves to hunt for food.
- While the female is gone, the male goes without food for nearly 2 months.
- The emperor penguin can dive to a depth of more than 1,500 ft (450 m).

CREATED KIND MEMBERS

All penguins

CLASS:	Aves (birds)
ORDER:	Sphenisciformes (penguins)
FAMILY:	Spheniscidae
GENUS/SPECIES:	*Aptenodytes forsteri*
Size:	Average almost 4 ft (1.2 m)
Weight:	42–101 lbs (19–46 kg)
Original Diet:	Plants
Present Diet:	Fish and crustaceans
Habitat:	In Antarctic waters; nests on ice floes or Antarctic mainland

EMU

EMU
CREATED ON DAY 5

DESIGN

The emu is designed to cope well with the extreme temperatures of its habitat. It has the ability to store fat after eating abundantly, which then allows it to survive during times when food is scarce. Young emus have black, brown, and cream stripes just after they hatch. This design gives them a better chance of survival since it blends them into their surroundings.

FEATURES

- The emu is smaller than the ostrich and is native to Australia.
- It has brown or grayish-black feathers, and brown legs, bill, and eyes. Its neck is blue.
- The emus is the second largest bird.

FUN FACTS

- The emu is Australia's national bird.
- The egg of the emu is normally a green color.
- The male is the one who incubates the egg.

CREATED KIND MEMBERS

Cassowary

CLASS:	Aves (birds)
ORDER:	Struthioniformes (ratites)
FAMILY:	Dromaiidae (emus)
GENUS/SPECIES:	*Dromaius novaehollandiae*
Size:	5–7 ft (1.8–2.1 m)
Weight:	Average: 110 lbs (50 kg)
Original Diet:	Plants
Present Diet:	Plants, insects, and small vertebrates
Habitat:	Savannas and open forests of Australia

FINCH

FINCH
CREATED ON DAY 5

DESIGN

The finch has been used by many to support the doctrine of evolution. Charles Darwin observed thirteen different species of finches on one island that had variations in shape and size of beak. He proposed that the different species evolved from one original pair, each adapting to its habitat and diet. But this is not evidence for molecules-to-man evolution, but rather an example of natural selection and adaptation. When God created the finch kind, He created it with all the necessary information it needed to survive in the wild. On the islands where Darwin observed them, they had adapted to their diet and their surroundings, resulting in several "different" varieties, which needed different beaks to eat different things in times of drought and in times of plenty.

FEATURES

- Finch beaks are cone-shaped and are used to break open seeds.
- Many species are brightly colored with red, blue, and yellow feathers while some others also have green.

FUN FACTS

- True finches usually have strong voices.
- They build cup-shaped nests, and goldfinches usually lay 5 pale-blue or greenish-blue eggs that will hatch in about 12 days. Babies will fledge about 12 days after that.

CREATED KIND MEMBERS

Goldfinch, grosbeak

CLASS:	Aves (birds)
ORDER:	Passeriformes (perching birds)
FAMILY:	Fringillidae (finches)
GENUS/SPECIES:	134 species in 19 genera
Size:	Mostly 4–6 in long (0.1–0.2 m)
Weight:	Only a few ounces (grams)
Original Diet:	Plants
Present Diet:	Primarily seed-eaters
Habitat:	All over the world except for Antarctica

FLAMINGO

FLAMINGO
CREATED ON DAY 5

DESIGN

The flamingo sucks water and mud into its beak with its unique tongue and then pumps the water out the sides of its mouth. Small creatures are captured in the flamingo's filtering system of tiny plates. Flamingos feed in a manner similar to that of baleen whales. Flamingos occur in flocks. This instinct given to them by their Creator, helps protect them from predators. In God's original creation, this instinct was not needed since all animals were vegetarian.

FEATURES

- The flamingo is known for its bright pink feathers and uniquiely downcurved black-tipped bill, which is adapted to filter feeding.
- It stands on its long legs to feed in shallow water, bending its neck and actually inserting its bill underwater in an upside down position. This is unique in the avian world.

FUN FACTS

- The flamingo's pink color comes from the food that it eats.
- The flamingo uses different displays including head-flagging, wing saluting, twist-preening, and marching.
- All five species of flamingos have black flight feathers.
- Flamingos can fly up to 35 mph (60 km/h).

CREATED KIND MEMBERS

Greater flamingo, lesser flamingo

CLASS:	Aves (birds)
ORDER:	Phoenicopteriformes (flamingos)
FAMILY:	Phoenicopteridae
GENUS/SPECIES:	Five separate species
Size:	About 3–5 ft (1–1.6 m) tall; wingspan: 3–5 ft (1–1.6 m)
Weight:	Between 3 and 9 lbs (1.5–4.1 kg)
Original Diet:	Plants
Present Diet:	Algae, shrimp, and other small aquatic creatures
Habitat:	Africa, Asia, the Americas, and Europe in shallow lakes or lagoons

GREAT BLUE HERON

GREAT BLUE HERON
CREATED ON DAY 5

DESIGN

The long legs of a heron allow it to effectively fish in the wetland areas where it lives. A heron's bill is perfectly designed to catch its food. It use it to stab fish, which it then swallows whole. This feature was given by God and was adapted for the consumption of meat, sometime after the Fall of man.

FEATURES

- The great blue heron is the largest heron in North America.
- It has rounded wings and a long, pointed bill. The great blue heron has a gray upper body and neck. It also is streaked with white, black, and brown.

FUN FACTS

- A great blue heron swallows its food whole.
- Even though the great blue heron likes to hunt alone, it will sometimes sleep in groups of over 100.

CREATED KIND MEMBERS

Black-headed heron, great egret

CLASS:	Aves (birds)
ORDER:	Ciconiiformes (storks and relatives)
FAMILY:	Ardeidae (herons, egrets)
GENUS/SPECIES:	*Ardea herodias*
Size:	3–5 ft tall (1–1.4 m)
Weight:	4–5 lbs (2.1–2.5 kg)
Original Diet:	Plants
Present Diet:	Fish mainly, but also frogs, salamanders, and other water creatures
Habitat:	Wetland areas around lakes, ponds, and rivers in most of North and Central America and northern South America

GREAT HORNED OWL

GREAT HORNED OWL
CREATED ON DAY 5

DESIGN

The great horned owl has excellent night vision and special adaptations to its flight feathers, which make its flight noiseless. These features make the owl a proficient hunter at night, which became a necessary ability after the Fall. Since owls' eyes are positioned in the front of their heads, they do not have binocular vision behind them as many other birds do. However, they were designed with the ability to turn their heads almost 270 degrees.

FEATURES

- The great horned owl is large and has ear tufts on its head and a white patch on its throat.
- The female is generally larger than the male.
- The great horned owl is the fiercest species of owl in North America.

FUN FACTS

- The great horned owl is mostly nocturnal, hunting and eating during the night and sleeping during the day.
- Female and male owls will sing "love" songs when in the mating season.
- Owls cannot turn their heads all the way around, as is commonly believed.
- This species is recognized by its call "Who, who."

CREATED KIND MEMBERS

All owls

CLASS:	Aves (birds)
ORDER:	Strigiformes (owls)
FAMILY:	Strigidae (typical owls)
GENUS/SPECIES:	*Bubo virginianus*
Size:	Between 18–25 in (0.5–0.6 m); Wingspan up to 4.5 ft (1.4 m)
Weight:	2–4 lbs (0.9–1.8 kg)
Original Diet:	Plants
Present Diet:	Amphibians, reptiles, birds, and mammals; mostly rodents
Habitat:	The Americas—North, Central, and South; in woodlands adjacent to open areas

GREATER ROADRUNNER

GREATER ROADRUNNER
CREATED ON DAY 5

DESIGN

The greater roadrunner is adapted to its desert home by being able to lower its body temperature at night, which conserves energy and conserves water during dry spells. The roadrunner's feet are also well designed for running on the hard ground. Two toes point forward while the other two point backward.

FEATURES

- The greater roadrunner has a dark brown, streaked appearance with lighter brown on its breast. It is also easily recognized by its bare red and blue skin on the head and bluish beak.

FUN FACTS

- The greater roadrunners is a better runner than flier. So, generally it will fly only when absolutely necessary.
- It can run up to 17 mph (27 km/h), and is quick enough to catch rattlesnakes.
- The greater roadrunner likes to sunbathe.
- It is the state bird of New Mexico. It was adopted under the name "chaparral bird."

CREATED KIND MEMBERS

Ground cuckoo

CLASS:	Aves (birds)
ORDER:	Cuculiformes (cuckoos, hoatzin, and relatives)
FAMILY:	Cuculidae (cuckoos, roadrunners, and relatives)
GENUS/SPECIES:	*Geococcyx californianus*
Size:	19–25 in (0.5–0.6 m)
Weight:	8–12 oz (0.2–0.3 kg)
Original Diet:	Plants
Present Diet:	Insects, lizards, snakes, mice, and sometimes other birds
Habitat:	North American deserts and tall pines in East Texas

HUMBOLT PENGUIN

HUMBOLDT PENGUIN
CREATED ON DAY 5

DESIGN

The humboldt penguin has claws on the toes of its webbed feet. These claws help the penguin climb the rocky terrain of its habitat. Some evolutionists say that the flippers of this penguin evolved from wings; however, we know that God designed the penguin to be an excellent swimmer. The Humboldt penguin has flipper-like wings because that is what God intended it to have.

FEATURES

- Like the emperor penguin, the Humboldt penguin also wears its black and white suit, but the pattern is different.
- The Humboldt penguin is also much smaller than the emperor penguin.
- It has pink around its eyes and on its beak.

FUN FACTS

- Each Humboldt penguin (like all other penguin species) has a distinctly different voice; this allows parents and their offspring to find each other in a crowd.
- This species can drink both saltwater and freshwater.

CREATED KIND MEMBERS

All penguins

CLASS:	Aves (birds)
ORDER:	Sphenisciformes (penguins)
FAMILY:	Spheniscidae
GENUS/SPECIES:	*Spheniscus humboldti*
Size:	25–27 in (0.6–0.7 m)
Weight:	About 9 lbs (4 kg)
Original Diet:	Plants
Present Diet:	Fish and squid
Habitat:	Marine along coasts of Peru and Chile in South America

HUMMINGBIRD

HUMMINGBIRD
CREATED ON DAY 5

DESIGN

God designed the bill of the hummingbird to be a long, slender tube. This allows the bird to go deep into flowers to extract the nectar. It also has a long tongue that is curled on its edges, forming two trays to collect the nectar. When the bird has collected the nectar, it will retract its tongue and squeeze the nectar into its throat. North American hummingbirds migrate long distances, some crossing the Gulf of Mexico.

FEATURES

- Hummingbirds are known for their long bills, dazzling colors, and speedy wings.
- Hummingbirds are the smallest birds in the world, and the smallest hummingbird is the bee hummingbird, which occurs in Cuba and the Isle of Pines. It weighs approximately 0.06 ounces (1.6 g), less than a U.S. penny.

FUN FACTS

- One species of hummingbird can fly up to 93 mph (150 km/h) during short chase flights, but they can beat their wings even faster, up to 200 times per second.
- A hummingbird takes in an incredible amount of calories daily. If humans ate the same amount as a hummingbird, we would have to ingest almost 155,000 calories a day. That's 77 times more than most humans eat.
- Hummingbirds are like helicopters; they can go up, down, forward, backward, and side to side with great precision.

CREATED KIND MEMBERS

Purple-crowned fairy, red-tailed comet, green-throated mango

CLASS:	Aves (birds)
ORDER:	Apodiformes (unfooted birds)
FAMILY:	Trochilidae (hummingbirds)
GENUS/SPECIES:	328 species
Size:	Largest: 8.6 in (0.2 m); Smallest: 2 in (0.05 m)
Weight:	0.06–0.7 oz. (1.6–21 grams)
Original Diet:	Plants
Present Diet:	Nectar and occasionally insects
Habitat:	An extremely wide range of habitats in North, Central, and South America

MACAW

MACAW
CREATED ON DAY 5

DESIGN

The large, curved beak of the macaw is designed to crush nuts and seeds. Some macaws have been observed to file down the shell of nuts and seeds by rubbing them on their beaks. This allows them to break the shell more easily. These birds are seldom seen alone. They spend time in pairs, family groups, and flocks. This behavior protects them from predators.

FEATURES

- Macaws are known for their large, curved beaks; loud, squawking calls; and bright, bold colors.
- Macaws are very social birds, living in flocks of 10 to 30 other individuals.

FUN FACTS

- The macaw's tongue is dry and scaly and has a bone in it. This makes it useful in eating and breaking open its food.
- The macaw can easily break a person's knuckle with its beak.

CREATED KIND MEMBERS

Scarlet macaw, yellow-headed parrot

CLASS:	Aves (birds)
ORDER:	Psittaciformes (parrots)
FAMILY:	Psittacidae (parrot)
GENUS/SPECIES:	17 different species
Size:	Largest: 3 ft (1 m); Smallest: almost 1 ft (0.3 m)
Weight:	Largest: 3–4 lbs (1.4–1.7 kg); Smallest: 9–10 oz (0.3 kg)
Original Diet:	Plants
Present Diet:	Fruits, nuts, seeds, flowers, leaves, snails, and insects
Habitat:	Rainforests, seasonally flooded savanna and palm forests; Central and South America

OSPREY

OSPREY
CREATED ON DAY 5

DESIGN

The osprey is designed with long, curved, and very sharp claws. These claws, as well as its reversible outer toe, give the osprey the ability to grip its prey. The information for these features was part of God's original creation, but the use of these features to catch prey was not necessary until after the Fall. The osprey also has nasal valves that prevent water from entering the bird's nostrils when it dives into the water to catch fish.

FEATURES

- The osprey is a large bird with a white underbelly and neck, brown body, dark eye lines, black beak, and bluish feet. There are slight variations within each subspecies.

FUN FACTS

- After an osprey catches a fish, it turns the prey so it faces forward. This is believed to make it easier to carry while flying.
- The male osprey will "sky-dance" when trying to attract a mate.

CREATED KIND MEMBERS

Eagles

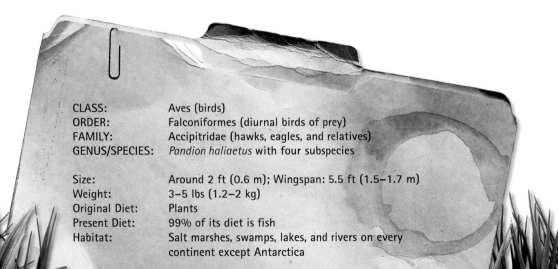

CLASS:	Aves (birds)
ORDER:	Falconiformes (diurnal birds of prey)
FAMILY:	Accipitridae (hawks, eagles, and relatives)
GENUS/SPECIES:	*Pandion haliaetus* with four subspecies
Size:	Around 2 ft (0.6 m); Wingspan: 5.5 ft (1.5–1.7 m)
Weight:	3–5 lbs (1.2–2 kg)
Original Diet:	Plants
Present Diet:	99% of its diet is fish
Habitat:	Salt marshes, swamps, lakes, and rivers on every continent except Antarctica

OSTRICH

OSTRICH
CREATED ON DAY 5

DESIGN

Because of the desert environment where the ostrich lives, it has the ability to store enough water to go for months without drinking. An ostrich will eat rocks to help with digestion. How would the ostrich know that this would help it without the designed instinct given by its Creator?

FEATURES

- Males are black with white wing and tail feathers, while the females have a brown plumage with wings and tail a dirty white.
- The ostrich is the largest living bird in the world.

FUN FACTS

- Ostrich eggshells are so hard that a grown man can stand on one without breaking it.
- An ostrich can run up to 40 mph (64 km/h) to escape its predators or give them a swift kick which could kill them.
- Ostrich fossils have been found in Europe and Asia.

CREATED KIND MEMBERS

Masai ostrich, Arabian ostrich

CLASS:	Aves (birds)
ORDER:	Struthioniformes (ratites)
FAMILY:	Struthionidae (ostriches)
GENUS/SPECIES:	*Struthio camelus*
Size:	Close to 9 ft (2.8 m)
Weight:	Up to 345 lbs (157 kg)
Original Diet:	Plants
Present Diet:	Vegetation and sometimes lizards
Habitat:	African plains, over much of the continent

PEAFOWL

PEAFOWL
CREATED ON DAY 5

DESIGN

The tail feathers of the peafowl are used to attract a mate and to ward off enemies. The "eyes" on the tips of its feathers can scare off predators; however, it did not need to ward off predators until after the Fall of man. Because of the peafowl's beauty, many explorers and voyagers captured these animals and took them to their homes. The peafowl's display of tail feathers is actually designed with remarkable precision. Every detail within each feather coordinates exactly to give us the eye pattern and fan-shape of the peafowl's tail.

FEATURES

- The peafowl is the largest member of the pheasant family.
- The male, with his metallic blue head, neck, and upper body, is more brightly colored than the female.

FUN FACTS

- Most people call the peafowl a "peacock," but the peacock is actually a male peafowl. The female is called a "peahen."
- The peafowl has an average of 200 tail feathers, which are shed every year in the fall and regrown in December or January.
- When in groups, the peafowl will warn each other of coming danger by shrieking cries and honks.

CREATED KIND MEMBERS

Turkey, ptarmigan

CLASS:	Aves (birds)
ORDER:	Galliformes (chicken-like birds)
FAMILY:	Phasianidae (pheasants, quail and relatives)
GENUS/SPECIES:	*Pavo cristatus* and *P. muticus* (blue [also called Indian] and green)
Size:	Up to over 7 ft (2.1 m) long; almost 5 ft (1.5 m) is tail
Weight:	Between 6 and 8.8 lbs (2.7–4 kg)
Original Diet:	Plants
Present Diet:	Small plants and animals, including snakes
Habitat:	Open deciduous forests near streams in Pakistan, India, and Sri Lanka

PEREGRINE FALCON

PEREGRINE FALCON
CREATED ON DAY 5

DESIGN

As with other birds of flight, the falcon is designed with hollow bones, a lightweight beak, and air sacs that connect to the airway. These design features along with its feathers and wing structure make it a capable flyer. The peregrine falcon may teach its young to hunt by dropping dead prey to its flying young who then must grasp it while in flight. This was not part of their behavior until after the Fall of man.

FEATURES

- The adult peregrine has bluish gray wings, a pale underbelly, and a black head.
- Immature peregrine falcons tend to be darker and browner in color.

FUN FACTS

- The peregrine falcon may migrate distances greater than 15,500 miles (25,000 km).
- Nests of these falcons have been seen on tall buildings even in cities. They prefer to place them at great heights, mostly on cliffs.
- The peregrine falcon can reach speeds up to 200 mph (322 km/h) when diving after its prey.

CREATED KIND MEMBERS

Prairie falcon, American kestrel

CLASS:	Aves (birds)
ORDER:	Falconiformes (diurnal birds of prey)
FAMILY:	Falconidae (falcons)
GENUS/SPECIES:	*Falco peregrinus*
Size:	Wingspan: between 3 and 4 ft (1–1.1 m)
Weight:	Average 2 lbs (0.9 kg)
Original Diet:	Plants
Present Diet:	Primarily smaller birds, but also small mammals and insects
Habitat:	Found in open country near cliffs, on all continents except for Antarctica

PILEATED WOODPECKER

PILEATED WOODPECKER
CREATED ON DAY 5

DESIGN

The woodpecker is designed with small tufts of feathers covering its nostrils. These feathers keep debris from getting into its nostrils while it is pecking away at tree bark. A woodpecker can peck holes into trees without getting a headache because it is designed with a "cushion" in its head, which is actually a special muscle that absorbs the shock of the bill pounding the tree. Without this design feature the woodpecker would not be able to remove the bark of trees to find food.

FEATURES

- The pileated woodpecker is known for the bright red crests on its head.
- This woodpecker's body is black with white stripes along the neck up to the head.

FUN FACTS

- Woodpeckers do not eat the bark of trees; they peck at it and remove it to find beetle larvae and other insects underneath.
- Some woodpeckers have tongues with barbs, which can spear prey. Others have sticky tongues, which cause invertebrate prey to adhere to it.

CREATED KIND MEMBERS

Imperial woodpecker, red-necked woodpecker

CLASS:	Aves (birds)
ORDER:	Piciformes (woodpeckers and relatives)
FAMILY:	Picidae (woodpeckers)
GENUS/SPECIES:	*Dryocopus pileatus*
Size:	16.5 in (0.4 m) long; wingspan average 29 in (0.7 m)
Weight:	10 oz (0.3 kg)
Original Diet:	Plants
Present Diet:	Insects
Habitat:	Mature forests of Canada and the eastern United States

PUFFIN

PUFFIN
CREATED ON DAY 5

DESIGN

The puffin is designed with a sharp hook in its bills, which helps it hold fish. This feature became a vital part of the puffin's survival after the Fall, when animals began to eat other animals. This bird has a special gland that produces a special oil that repels water from its feathers. The puffin's feathers are also designed to trap air in them, which provides it with extra heat.

FEATURES

- This bird, like a penguin, stands vertically and has black and white coloring. However, the shape of its brightly-colored bill distinguishes it from the penguin.

FUN FACTS

- Although this bird looks similar to a penguin, it is probably a distinct kind.
- A puffin can fly at speeds up to 40 mph (64 km/h).
- Puffins occur in the Northern Hemisphere, wile penguins occur in the Southern Hemisphere.

CREATED KIND MEMBERS

Auklet, murrelet

CLASS:	Aves (birds)
ORDER:	Charadriiformes (shore-birds and relatives)
FAMILY:	Alcidae (auks)
GENUS/SPECIES:	*Fratercula arctica, F. cirrhata* and *F. corniculata* (Atlantic, tufted, and horned)
Size:	12.5–15 in (0.3–0.4 m)
Weight:	About 1 lb (0.5 kg)
Original Diet:	Plants
Present Diet:	Fish and aquatic invertebrates
Habitat:	North Atlantic and Pacific oceans, nesting on rocky coasts and offshore islands

SNOWY OWL

SNOWY OWL
CREATED ON DAY 5

DESIGN

The powerful and sharp talons of the snowy owl enable it to clutch and capture small prey. This feature would not have been needed until after the Fall of man when animals became carnivores. The feet of the snowy owl are feathered, which protects it from the cold weather of its habitat.

FEATURES

- The snowy owl is one of the largest owls; the female is noticeably larger than the male.
- It has a white body with a black beak and yellow eyes. The female has blackish spots while the male is mostly pure white.
- The snowy owl is more agile than other owls and is able to capture birds while in flight.

FUN FACTS

- The snowy owl protects its young from predators by pretending to have a broken wing and leading them away from its nest.
- A male will sometimes present a prospective mate with a dead animal as a gift.

CREATED KIND MEMBERS

All owls

CLASS:	Aves (birds)
ORDER:	Strigiformes (owls)
FAMILY:	Strigidae (typical owls)
GENUS/SPECIES:	*Nyctea scandiaca*
Size:	Average close to 2 ft (0.5–0.7 m); wingspan averages 4.3 ft (1.3 m)
Weight:	Between 4 and 6 lbs (1.8–2.9 kg)
Original Diet:	Plants
Present Diet:	Rodents and birds
Habitat:	Tundra regions of North America and Eurasia

TRUMPETER SWAN

TRUMPETER SWAN
CREATED ON DAY 5

DESIGN

God designed a preen gland on the lower back at the base of the tail of the trumpeter swan (and most other birds) to store an oily fluid that waterproofs, cleans, and protects its feathers. The swan covers its feathers with this oily secretion when it preens them with its beak. The adult swan will molt all its feathers once a year, during the warmest months of the year. This timing reflects the design of its Creator.

FEATURES

- The trumpeter swan is known for its white plumage and black bill.
- It is the largest species of waterfowl in North America.
- Its bill contains fine, tooth-like serrations along the edges that strain water when the bird eats aquatic vegetation.

FUN FACTS

- The trumpeter swan gets its name from the call it makes.
- For approximately a month, the trumpeter swan will be completely flightless because it molts all of its flight feathers at the same time.
- Baby swans are called cygnets.
- By 1900, this species was thought to be extinct, but a small remnant population was found in Montana, Idaho, and Wyoming. The species is slowly recovering with the help of conservation biologists.

CREATED KIND MEMBERS

Duck, goose

CLASS:	Aves (birds)
ORDER:	Anseriformes (waterfowl)
FAMILY:	Anatidae (ducks, geese, and swans)
GENUS/SPECIES:	*Cygnus buccinator*
Size:	Wingspan 6–8 ft (1.8–2.4 m); around 4 ft (1.2 m) tall
Weight:	21–26 lbs (9.5–12.5 kg); Males are larger than females
Original Diet:	Plants
Present Diet:	Almost entirely vegetarian (aquatic plants, seeds, tubers); Cygnets eat aquatic invertebrates at first
Habitat:	Waters in boreal forest zones in North America; mainly western Canada and western U.S.

TOCO TOUCAN

TOCO TOUCAN
CREATED ON DAY 5

DESIGN

The bright colors of the Toco may seem to us to make it stand out; however, God designed it with those bright colors as part of His creativity and beauty in creation. Since the Fall of man, these colors seem to help this species blend into its habitat. Its dark body allows it to hide in the shadows of trees and its bright colors are easily overlooked as flowers or fruit among the trees. Even though its beak appears heavy, it is actually designed with lightweight material, containing a number of air pockets.

FEATURES

- The body plumage of the Toco toucan is black with a white patch on its throat. The beak of the Toco is brightly colored while bare orange areas surround the eyes.
- The Toco is the only non-forest toucan.

FUN FACTS

- Thin rods of bone help support the Toco's beak.
- The Toco's tongue is similar to a feather, and it is used to toss food down its throat.
- With such a large bill, the toucan has a unique sleeping position. It turns its head around and lays its bill on its back.
- Tocos participate in a ritual of tossing fruit to each other.

CREATED KIND MEMBERS

Keel-billed toucan, white-throated toucan

CLASS:	Aves (birds)
ORDER:	Piciformes (woodpeckers and relatives)
FAMILY:	Ramphastidae (toucan)
GENUS/SPECIES:	*Ramphastos toco*
Size:	About 25 in (0.6 m) long; beak up to 7.5 in (0.2 m)
Weight:	About 18–30 oz (0.5–0.8 kg)
Original Diet:	Plants
Present Diet:	Fruit and some insects; occasionally, birds, lizards, and eggs
Habitat:	Mainly riverine edges of forest and forest patches in savannas in eastern and central South America

WHITE-TAILED PTARMIGAN

WHITE-TAILED PTARMIGAN
CREATED ON DAY 5

DESIGN

The white-tailed ptarmigan molts twice a year, once in the spring and once in the fall. When it molts in the fall, its new feathers are white, but when it molts again in the spring, its new feathers are brown. This allows the ptarmigan to blend into its surroundings all year round. This species also knows how to adapt to colder weather. Some of its habits include hiding in rock piles or even pockets under the snow.

FEATURES

- All three species of ptarmigans are rather round birds with variously mottled brown, black, and gray plumage in the summer, a black beak, and feathered feet.
- The white-tailed ptarmigan has white tail feathers, while the other two species of ptarmigan have black tail feathers.

FUN FACTS

- The ptarmigan has feathers on its feet to help it walk on the snow.
- This bird likes to walk more than it does to fly.
- It eats grit to help it digest its food.

CREATED KIND MEMBERS

Willow ptarmigan, rock ptarmigan

CLASS:	Aves (birds)
ORDER:	Galliformes (chicken-like birds)
FAMILY:	Tetraonidae (grouse)
GENUS/SPECIES:	*Lagopus leucurus*
Size:	11–16 in (0.3 m)
Weight:	Average less than 1 lb (0.5 kg)
Original Diet:	Plants
Present Diet:	Plants and insects
Habitat:	Alpine meadows and rocky areas at or above the tree line, from Alaska to northern Washington, Montana, and the Rocky Mountain states

WILD TURKEY

WILD TURKEY
CREATED ON DAY 5

DESIGN

The wings of the wild turkey are large and rounded, and even though the ratio of body weight to wing area is one of the highest in any birds, they are powerful enough for the turkey to reach speeds up to 55 mph (89 km/h). This design enables the turkey to escape danger when threatened by a predator. When disturbed, the turkey prefers to run rather than fly.

FEATURES

- The trukey is known for its round body, fan-shaped tail, long neck, and large size.
- The male has a red wattle that hangs from the side of the head and a caruncle on its forehead.
- The male also has a red, blue, or white head, which is different from the gray-headed female.

FUN FACTS

- A male turkey's gobble can be heard up to a mile away.
- Even though the turkey spends most of its time on the ground, it roosts in trees with other members of its flock.
- Benjamin Franklin wanted the turkey to be the national bird of the U.S.

CREATED KIND MEMBERS

Ocellated turkey, peafowl

CLASS:	Aves (birds)
ORDER:	Galliformes (chicken-like birds)
FAMILY:	Meleagrididae
GENUS/SPECIES:	*Meleagris gallopavo*
Size:	3–4 ft (0.9–1.2 m) from head to tail
Weight:	8–22 lbs (3.6–10 kg)
Original Diet:	Plants
Present Diet:	Plants, insects, and salamanders
Habitat:	Forests

BOBCAT

BOBCAT
CREATED ON DAY 6

DESIGN

In spite of its small size, the bobcats is a ferocious predator. It has the ability to kill an animal as large as a deer. The female bobcat teaches her young to hunt two weeks after they are born. If the bobcat makes a big kill, it will drag its prey to a safe location, eat what it desires, and then cover up the rest to return later to feed. This allows it to feed a number of times on a single kill. These predatory skills became part of the bobcat's instincts after the Fall of man.

FEATURES

- The bobcat can be distinguished from other cats by its ear tufts and ruffs of hair on the sides its face. Its fur is mainly brown and beige with darker shades making up the spots. The backs of its ears are black, and the tip of its tail has black bars on it.

FUN FACTS

- Unlike other cats, the bobcat's tail is relatively short. This is possibly where it gets its name.
- The bobcat likes to live and hunt alone.
- The growl of the bobcat is easily confused with the growl of a mountain lion.
- The bobcat is the most common wildcat in North America.

CREATED KIND MEMBERS

Cheetah, jaguar, leopard, lion, tiger, cougar, housecat, lynx

CLASS:	Mammalia (mammal)
ORDER:	Carnivora (meat-eating)
FAMILY:	Felidae (cat kind)
GENUS/SPECIES:	*Lynx rufus*
Size:	25–41 in (0.6–1 m)
Weight:	8–33 lbs (4–15 kg)
Original Diet:	Plants
Present Diet:	Rodents, rabbits, birds, and reptiles
Habitat:	Occurs in a wide variety of habitats from the Atlantic to the Pacific ocean and from Mexico to southern British Columbia

CHEETAH

CHEETAH
CREATED ON DAY 6

DESIGN

The cheetah has smaller teeth than the other large cats. It has large, powerful claws that help grab the ground at high speeds, and larger nasal passages that allow it to take in more air during and after running. These physical features began to be used to kill prey after man's disobedience against God.

FEATURES

- The cheetah is known by its distinct spots and white patches on its stomach.
- Its spots are round or oval and usually measure about an inch in diameter.

FUN FACTS

- The cheetah is the fastest land mammal, reaching speeds up to 70 mph (113 km/h).
- It can turn in midair while sprinting after its prey.
- Genetically, cheetah populations are nearly 100% homozygous. The only other known populations like this are the white lab rats and lab mice, which are artificially bred to have this genetic quality.

CREATED KIND MEMBERS

Bobcat, jaguar, leopard, lion, tiger, cougar, housecat

CLASS:	Mammalia (mammal)
ORDER:	Carnivora (meat-eating)
FAMILY:	Felidae (cat kind)
GENUS/SPECIES:	*Acinonyx jubatus*
Size:	2–3 ft (0.7–0.9 m) tall; around 4 ft (1.4 m) long
Weight:	110–143 lbs (50–65 kg)
Original Diet:	Plants
Present Diet:	Antelope, birds, rabbits, and porcupines
Habitat:	Grasslands and savannas of Africa and eastward to India

COUGAR

COUGAR
CREATED ON DAY 6

DESIGN

Even though the cougar is found in few places in North America, it plays an important role in its habitat by keeping other animals in check. This carnivorous behavior was not part of its original created kind but came after the Fall. The cougar will sometimes hide its large prey and return to eat it later. This allows it to thrive even when the food supply is low.

FEATURES

- The cougar is yellowish-brown in color with a whitish chest.
- It has large golden eyes, a pink nose, and a long, cylindrical tail.

FUN FACTS

- The puma and the mountain lion are the same thing as a cougar. Many also call the cougar a panther, but some disagree with this naming of the species.
- A cougar cannot roar; it has a unique scream.
- It can jump up to 18 ft (5.5 m) from a sitting position.
- A cougar needs a hunting territory of up to 300 square miles (780 km^2).

CREATED KIND MEMBERS

Cheetah, jaguar, leopard, lion, tiger, bobcat, housecat

CLASS:	Mammalia (mammal)
ORDER:	Carnivora (meat-eating)
FAMILY:	Felidae (cat kind)
GENUS/SPECIES:	*Puma concolor*
Size:	3–5 ft (0.9–1.5 m) tall
Weight:	77–230 lbs (35–105 kg)
Original Diet:	Plants
Present Diet:	Deer, rabbits, moose, beaver, bobcats, and other mammals
Habitat:	Forests, grasslands, mountains, and deserts from British Columbia to Patagonia in South America

JAGUAR

JAGUAR
CREATED ON DAY 6

DESIGN

To catch fish, the jaguar will attract them by tapping the surface of the water with its tail. It also has powerful jaws that are used to puncture the skull of its prey and to break the spine of smaller prey. These behaviors of the jaguar developed after the Fall since they were created as vegetarians.

FEATURES

- The jaguar is the largest species of cat in the Western Hemisphere.
- The background of the jaguar's coat is a tawny-yellow, which lightens to whitish on the throat and belly. It is marked with small spots on the head and neck, and dark open ring structures, called rosettes, on the sides and flank that generally contain one to four dark spots inside the rings.

FUN FACTS

- A jaguar will follow its prey into the water.
- It also may capture its prey by leaping onto it from trees.
- Some jaguars can be black.

CREATED KIND MEMBERS

Cheetah, bobcat, leopard, lion, tiger, cougar, housecat

CLASS:	Mammalia (mammal)
ORDER:	Carnivora (meat-eating)
FAMILY:	Felidae (cat kind)
GENUS/SPECIES:	*Panthera onca*
Size:	5–6 ft (1.5–1.8 m) long; 27–30 in (0.7–2 m) tall
Weight:	150–300 lbs (68–136 kg); Females are generally smaller.
Original Diet:	Plants
Present Diet:	Deer, monkeys, birds, reptiles, fish, amphibians, and other small mammals
Habitat:	Grasslands and forests from the southwestern U.S. into South America

LEOPARD

LEOPARD
CREATED ON DAY 6

DESIGN

After killing its prey, the leopard may drag the carcass up a tree to keep it from being eaten by other predators. It is possible that the information for this behavior was given to it by its Creator, but did not become part of its lifestyle until after the Fall. The fur on leopards living in colder regions is thicker than the fur of those living in tropical regions.

FEATURES

- The leopard's coat has a background color of pale cream on its underside that darkens slightly to an orange-brown on its back. Solid black spots adorn the limbs and head, while larger rosettes cover its back and sides.
- A leopard has broad feet and small ears.
- This species can also be completely black.

FUN FACTS

- The leopard is very hard to spot in the wild. Sometimes it can sneak up directly next to its prey without being noticed.
- All leopard populations are threatened or endangered.

CREATED KIND MEMBERS

Cheetah, jaguar, bobcat, lion, tiger, cougar, housecat

CLASS:	Mammalia (mammal)
ORDER:	Carnivora (meat-eating)
FAMILY:	Felidae (cat kind)
GENUS/SPECIES:	*Panthera pardus*
Size:	5–8 ft (1–1.5 m) long; Between 1–2 ft (0.3–.06 m) tall
Weight:	200 lbs (91 kg)
Original Diet:	Plants
Present Diet:	Birds, rabbits, rodents, monkeys, fish, reptiles, antelope, and jackals
Habitat:	Deserts, forests, and savannas of Africa and Asia

LION

LION
CREATED ON DAY 6

DESIGN

Lions live in groups called prides. These prides make hunting a group effort although lions do hunt alone or in pairs, as well. Prides also provide the young with a greater survival rate since there is more than one female to provide food and protection for the cubs. During World War II, lions in the zoo survived on plants since meat was rationed. This goes back prior to the Fall when all animals were vegetarians.

FEATURES

- Both male and female lions are tan; but only the male develops a mane. The mane is usually a darker brown color and helps protect the male from competitors in a fight.

FUN FACTS

- A lion can leap up to 36 ft (11 m) in one bound.
- Adult lions do not have any predators, except for man.
- Each lion has a unique pattern of whiskers on its muzzle.
- Lions take readily to water and are strong swimmers.

CREATED KIND MEMBERS

Cheetah, jaguar, leopard, bobcat, tiger, cougar, housecat

CLASS:	Mammalia (mammal)
ORDER:	Carnivora (meat-eating)
FAMILY:	Felidae (cat kind)
GENUS/SPECIES:	*Panthera leo*
Size:	About 4 ft (1.2 m) tall; 8–12 ft (2.4–3.7 m) long with tail
Weight:	Male: 300–550 lbs (150–250 kg); Female: 260–400 lbs (120–180 kg)
Original Diet:	Plants
Present Diet:	Wildebeest, zebra, and antelope; sometimes rhinoceros, elephant, or hippopotamus
Habitat:	Savanna and forests of Africa

TIGER

TIGER
CREATED ON DAY 6

DESIGN

Tigers were designed with longer hindlimbs than forelimbs, which allow them to leap. Ever since the Fall, they have used their powerful forelimbs to drag down prey while they use their hindlimbs to jump onto their prey. These limbs also make them very powerful swimmers. They can cross rivers that are up to 5 miles (8 km) wide.

FEATURES

- Tigers are easily distinguished from other large cats by their black stripes against their orange and tan backgrounds and white underbellies. Some Siberian tigers have white backgrounds and are considered a subspecies of *Panthera tigris*. These tigers live in Manchuria and Siberia.

FUN FACTS

- No two tigers have the same stripe pattern.
- Tigers communicate with each other by rubbing heads, roaring, purring, and grunting.
- A tiger can eat up to 85 lbs (39 kg) of meat at one sitting.

CREATED KIND MEMBERS

Cheetah, jaguar, leopard, lion, bobcat, cougar, housecat

CLASS:	Mammalia (mammal)
ORDER:	Carnivora (meat-eating)
FAMILY:	Felidae (cat kind)
GENUS/SPECIES:	*Panthera tigris* (contains 5 subspecies)
Size:	3 ft (0.9 m) tall; 5–12 ft (1.5–3.7 m) long with tail
Weight:	500–600 lbs (227–272 kg)
Original Diet:	Plants
Present Diet:	Mainly large animals such as deer, buffalo, and wild pigs
Habitat:	Siberia and the jungles of India, southern China, Malay Peninsula, and Sumatra

BABOON

BABOON
CREATED ON DAY 6

DESIGN

Baboons are social animals. They live in large groups called troops, normally consisting of one dominant male and numerous females. The troop gives the young a good chance of survival. Baboons are omnivores but are able to survive strictly on vegetation, which is how they were originally designed.

FEATURES

- Depending on the species, the baboon can vary in color from yellow to red and gray to black.
- Some species also have brightly-colored muzzles as well as colored rumps.
- Males have large upper canines which are displayed in defense and attack.

FUN FACTS

- Baboons groom each other as part of their social behavior.
- One species of male baboon kidnaps a female from her family unit to begin another family unit. He nurtures and care for her until she reaches maturity.
- Baboons use gestures, lip-smacking, and facial expressions as well as vocal communication.

CREATED KIND MEMBERS

Mandrill, macaque

CLASS:	Mammalia (mammal)
ORDER:	Primates (monkeys)
FAMILY:	Cercopithecidae (Old World monkeys)
GENUS:	*Papio* (Five different species)
Size:	2–4 ft (0.6–1.2 m); varies within species
Weight:	30–90 lbs (14–41 kg); varies within species
Original Diet:	Plants
Present Diet:	Plants, grubs, insects, and small vertebrates
Habitat:	Savannah, open woodland, and hills in Africa

CHIMPANZEE

CHIMPANZEE
CREATED ON DAY 6

DESIGN

Chimpanzees have recently been classified in the same family as humans; however, they are two very different and separate creatures. God created man special and unique with the ability to communicate with his Creator. The chimp was designed to live in trees. With its long arms, which are 1.5 times longer than its height, it is designed to swing from branch to branch. Also, its opposable toes, allow it to grip the branches of trees with its feet as well.

FEATURES

- The chimpanzee is a type of ape. Apes differ from monkeys in that they do not have tails, and their arms are longer than their legs.
- The chimp's foot and hand bones are curved between the knuckles ... humans' are straight.

FUN FACTS

- Like some other animals, the chimp uses tools to help it get food.
- Chimps greet each other by kissing, embracing, and grunting. Chimps play by wrestling, tickling, and chasing each other.

CREATED KIND MEMBERS

Bonobo

CLASS:	Mammalia (mammal)
ORDER:	Primates (monkeys)
FAMILY:	Hominidae (great apes)
GENUS/SPECIES:	*Pan troglodytes*
Size:	Males: 3–4 ft (0.9–1.2 m); Females: 2–3 ft (0.6–0.9 m)
Weight:	Between 123 and 176 lbs (56–80 kg)
Original Diet:	Plants
Present Diet:	Mostly herbivorous; but will eat insects and meat
Habitat:	Tropical rainforests in Africa

GORILLA

GORILLA
CREATED ON DAY 6

DESIGN

The gorilla's arms are extremely long, enabling it to walk on all four limbs while keeping its head up. It is primarily terrestrial but is fully capable of climbing. Contrary to common belief, the gorilla is not afraid of water and will frequently wade in swamp forests in search of aquatic vegetation.

FEATURES

- The gorilla is the largest primate.
- It is known for its black fur, large browridge, large nostrils, and short muzzle.
- The dark hair on the back of one subspecies becomes silvery gray as it matures.

FUN FACTS

- Like the stripes on a tiger and the spots on a giraffe, no two gorillas have the same nose print.
- The male gorilla can consume up to 50 lbs (23 kg) of vegetation a day.
- A gorilla can laugh, smile, and purr.
- It walks on its knuckles in order to protect its sensitive fingertips and to raise its body for more effective visual scanning.
- When threatened, the male gorilla will stand upright and emit loud roars and grunts.

CREATED KIND MEMBERS

Western gorilla, eastern gorilla

CLASS:	Mammalia (mammal)
ORDER:	Primates (monkeys)
FAMILY:	Hominidae (great apes)
GENUS/SPECIES:	2 subspecies: *Gorilla gorilla gorilla* and *G. gorilla berengei* (western lowland and eastern)
Size:	Around 5 ft (1.5 m) when upright, 4 ft (1.2 m) in normal stance
Weight:	Average about 400 lbs (181 kg); Males are heavier than females
Original Diet:	Plants
Present Diet:	Mostly plants, but also insects
Habitat:	Forests of equatorial Africa

ORANGUTAN

ORANGUTAN
CREATED ON DAY 6

DESIGN

The orangutans has powerful hands and arms but weak feet. These features are characteristic of tree-dwelling animals. The orangutan learns most of its behaviors from its mother. This species sleeps in trees, building a nest among the branches.

FEATURES

- The orangutan is most recognized by its reddish-orange coloring.
- It has hook-shaped hands and feet that are perfect for living in trees.
- The male has large cheek pads.

FUN FACTS

- The orangutan cannot swim.
- At night it makes a new nest to sleep in, and sometimes it build canopies over its nests to protect it from the rain.
- It will also use branches to protect its face from honeybees when invading a hive.

CREATED KIND MEMBERS

Bornean orangutan, Sumatran orangutan

CLASS:	Mammalia (mammal)
ORDER:	Primates (monkeys)
FAMILY:	Hominidae (great ape kind)
GENUS/SPECIES:	*Pongo pygmaeus,* possibly including *P. abelii* (Sumatran)
Size:	Males: 3.2–4.5 ft (1–1.4 m); Females: 2.6–3.5 ft (0.8–1.1 m)
Weight:	Males average 200 lbs (90 kg); Females average 110 lbs (50 kg).
Original Diet:	Plants
Present Diet:	Plants, insects, young birds, and small mammals
Habitat:	Tropical rainforests of southeast Asia (on the islands of Borneo and Sumatra)

PYGMY MARMOSET

PYGMY MARMOSET
CREATED ON DAY 6

DESIGN

Younger marmosets will help care for the young of others in their group while waiting to establish families of their own. By doing this, they learn the necessary skills to care for their own young. The pygmy marmoset is an active, agile creature, which moves through the trees in an upright position. Its forelimbs are shorter than its hindlimbs and it often feeds while clinging upright to a trunk or branch.

FEATURES

- The pygmy marmoset is the smallest monkey in the world.
- It is recognized by its silky, gray coat with yellow streaks. The longer hair on its head and cheeks gives it the appearance of having a mane.
- Its coloration provides great camouflage for its life in the trees.

FUN FACTS

- The pygmy marmoset can rest by piercing its nails into trees, allowing it to relax.
- When a pygmy marmoset is frightened, it turns its head in all directions very quickly, with sudden, jerky movements.
- This species sleeps in tree holes or vine tangles.

CREATED KIND MEMBERS

Tamorin, silky marmoset, black-tailed marmoset

CLASS:	Mammalia (mammal)
ORDER:	Primates (monkeys)
FAMILY:	Callitrichidae (marmosets and tamarins)
GENUS/SPECIES:	*Callithrix pygmaea*
Size:	15 in (0.4 m) tail included
Weight:	4–7 oz (0.1–0.2 kg)
Original Diet:	Plants
Present Diet:	Primarily tree sap; also fruits, insects, birds' eggs, and small birds
Habitat:	The Upper Amazon, parts of Ecuador, northern Peru, Bolivia, and western Brazil

RING-TAILED LEMUR

RING-TAILED LEMUR
CREATED ON DAY 6

DESIGN

The ring-tailed lemur's eyesight is so keen that it can see in the dark. It is an important component of its environment's ecology because it often eats seasonal fruit, the seeds of which it does not digest. It then passes the seeds in its waste, which then take root and grow. This helps replenish the vegetation of the island of Madagascar, off the southeastern coast of Africa.

FEATURES

- The ring-tailed lemur is recognized by its long tail with distinctive black and white bands, which are unique among all the lemurs.
- Its body is mostly grey with white underparts. Its narrow face is white with black patches around the eyes, and a black muzzle.

FUN FACTS

- The ring-tailed lemur is the only true lemur that has scent glands, which it uses to mark its territory. Two opposing males will often have "stink-fights."
- Lemurs are known to sunbathe in the morning, sitting with legs extended to effectively draw in heat.
- This is one of 22 species of lemurs, all of which only occur on the island of Madagascar, off the eastern coast of Mozambique, Africa.

CREATED KIND MEMBERS

Black lemur, bamboo lemur

CLASS:	Mammalia (mammal)
ORDER:	Primates (monkeys)
FAMILY:	Lemuridae (lemurs)
GENUS/SPECIES:	*Lemur catta*
Size:	Around 40 in (1 m) with tail
Weight:	5–7 lbs (2–3 kg)
Original Diet:	Plants
Present Diet:	Plants and insects
Habitat:	Spiny desert, scrub, and dry forest of Madagascar

WHITE-CHEEKED GIBBON

WHITE-CHEEKED GIBBON
CREATED ON DAY 6

DESIGN

The white-cheeked gibbon has extremely dense fur, which protects it from the rain of its habitat. It also has extremely long hook-shaped hands and feet, which is the perfect design for its life in the trees. It was also created with opposable thumbs, which are excellent design features for tree life given to the gibbon by its Creator.

FEATURES

- The arms and legs of the white-cheeked gibbon are longer than other primates' limbs.
- The male white-cheeked gibbon is black, but the females turn a golden color as she ages.
- The male is recognized by the white patches on his cheeks.

FUN FACTS

- The white-cheeked gibbon is known for its morning call which keeps pairs together and warns other family units away from its territory.
- This species is able to leap up to 30 ft (9 m) between trees.
- The white-cheeked gibbon cannot swim.

CREATED KIND MEMBERS

Black-crested gibbon, silvery gibbon, lar gibbon

CLASS:	Mammalia (mammals)
ORDER:	Primates (monkeys)
FAMILY:	Hylobatidae (tree-dwellers)
GENUS/SPECIES:	*Hylobates leucogenys*
Size:	1.5–2 ft (0.5–0.6 m)
Weight:	Average: 13 lbs (5.7 kg)
Original Diet:	Plants
Present Diet:	Mostly plants; some invertebrates, young birds, and eggs
Habitat:	Rainforests of Southeastern Asia from sea level to about 1.5 mi (2.4 km) elevation

ALLIGATOR

ALLIGATOR
CREATED ON DAY 6

DESIGN
The American alligator has vertical pupils in its eyes. It is able to see well in the low light of night. The alligator has been known to eat just about anything found in its watery habitat, from paper trash to fish hooks and aluminum cans. The nostrils of an alligator are slightly elevated on its snout, allowing it to breathe while remaining completely submerged.

FEATURES
- The alligator is smaller, darker, and has a more rounded snout than the crocodile.
- It also prefers freshwater to the saltwater that crocodiles enjoy.

FUN FACTS
- An alligator's lower jaw is very weak in comparison to its upper jaw. That is how a circus performer can stick his head inside an alligator's mouth without fear of getting it bitten off.
- The name "alligator" comes from the Spanish word "el lagarto," meaning "lizard."
- Alligators living in water containing a lot of algae have a greenish hue to their hides.

CREATED KIND MEMBERS
Crocodile, caiman

CLASS:	Reptilia (reptiles)
ORDER:	Crocodylia (crocodiles, alligators, and relatives)
FAMILY:	Alligatoridae (alligators)
GENUS/SPECIES:	*Alligator mississippiensis* (American alligator), *A. sinensis* (Chinese alligator)
Size:	10–19 ft (3–5.8 m); Males are larger than females
Weight:	Up to 1,000 lbs (454 kg)
Original Diet:	Plants
Present Diet:	Young eat insects and plants; mature alligators eat fish, mammals, and reptiles
Habitat:	Aquatic areas in southern U.S. and the Yangtze River in China

BALL PYTHON

BALL PYTHON
CREATED ON DAY 6

DESIGN

The ball python hunts and captures its prey by following it into its burrow. It also uses its heat sensitivity to locate and capture its prey. These pits can detect very slight changes in temperature. All snakes are designed with the ability to disengage their lower jaw, enabling them to swallow their prey whole. While feeding, the ball python can still breathe since its windpipe is placed on the floor of its mouth. This ability became important after the Fall, since all animals were created as vegetarians.

FEATURES

- The ball python varies in its color and patterns. Some are reddish-brown while others are yellow. Some have stripes while others have spots and some even have both.
- This species is also known as the royal python.

FUN FACTS

- The ball python gets its name from its defensive posture. When it feels threatened, it will roll into a ball and tuck its head into the middle.
- The teeth of the ball python face the back of the snake's mouth, which helps the snake swallow its food.

CREATED KIND MEMBERS

Pigmy python, green tree python

CLASS:	Reptilia (reptiles)
ORDER:	Squamata (amphisbaenians, lizards, and snakes [scaly])
FAMILY:	Boidae (boas and pythons)
GENUS/SPECIES:	*Python regius*
Size:	4–6 ft (1.3–1.8 m); Females are larger than males
Weight:	2–4.5 lbs (1–2 kg)
Original Diet:	Plants
Present Diet:	Rodents
Habitat:	Savannas and forests of western Africa, especially in the rainforests from Ghana to Cameroon

BOA CONSTRICTOR

BOA CONSTRICTOR
CREATED ON DAY 6

DESIGN

The boa constrictor has a strong tail that can cling to tree branches, enabling it to swing by its tail from a tree and swat a bird from the air. The boa plays an important role in its habitat by keeping down the population of many small rodents. This function was developed after the Fall, since all animals were originally plant-eaters.

FEATURES

- The common boa has patterns of reddish-brown that are outlined in black on its pale body. These patterns are shaped like ovals, diamonds, or bats.
- The boa has very small fangs and no venom. It wraps its body around its victim and suffocates it to death.

FUN FACTS

- Some boas can change colors like a lizard.
- This snake has heat-sensitive scales, instead of heat-sensitive pits.
- The boa constrictor not only has color vision, it also has extended infra-red vision well beyond where humans can see. This enables it to sense temperature differences of less than 0.03°C, enabling it to find live targets in the dense forest.
- The female boa produces live offspring instead of laying eggs.

CREATED KIND MEMBERS

Python

CLASS:	Reptilia (reptiles)
ORDER:	Squamata (amphisbaenians, lizards, and snakes [scaly])
FAMILY:	Boidae (boas and pythons)
GENUS/SPECIES:	*Boa constrictor*
Size:	5–14 ft (1.6–4.3 m)
Weight:	60–100 lbs (27–45 kg)
Original Diet:	Plants
Present Diet:	Birds, lizards, rodents, and other small mammals
Habitat:	Forest, desert, grassland in Central and South America

CHAMELEON

CHAMELEON
CREATED ON DAY 6

DESIGN

The chameleon has the unique ability to move each eye in a different direction at the same time. It is designed with a very long and sticky tongue (some being longer than the entire length of its body). This tongue allows the chameleon to capture its food even from long distances. The shape of the chameleon is specially designed for its life in trees. With its coloration and shape, the chameleon can be mistaken for a leaf or branch.

FEATURES

- The chameleon is distinctly different from other lizards. It has hands and feet that are able to grip objects. It also has a tail that can be used as a fifth limb.
- The chameleon has a horn or crest on its head, while other lizards do not.

FUN FACTS

- The chameleon can rapidly change its color for both camouflage and as an "emotion" indicator.
- The body of the chameleon is almost entirely flat.

CREATED KIND MEMBERS

Dwarf chameleon, pygmy chameleon, leaf chameleon

CLASS:	Reptilia (reptiles)
ORDER:	Squamata (amphisbaenians, lizards, and snakes [scaly])
FAMILY:	Chamaeleonidae (Old World chameleons)
GENUS/SPECIES:	More than 120 species
Size:	Less than 1 in to 27 in (0.03–0.7 m)
Weight:	Varies greatly
Original Diet:	Plants
Present Diet:	Insects
Habitat:	Tropical and mountainous rainforests, savannas, and steppes of northern Africa, the Middle East, India, and Madagascar

COMMON SNAPPING TURTLE

COMMON SNAPPING TURTLE
CREATED ON DAY 6

DESIGN

The snapping turtle is known as a scavenger. It will also prey on diseased fish and the young of ducks and other waterfowl. However, it was originally a plant-eater; this changed after the Fall. This species is designed with webbed feet, making it an excellent swimmer.

FEATURES

- The common snapping turtle can vary in color from black to tan. Its tail can reach or even surpass the length of its body.
- The snapping turtle is not an aggressive animal by nature; however, it will snap when it feels threatened, especially while it is on land.

FUN FACTS

- The common snapping turtle will bury itself in mud with just its eyes and nostrils sticking out, to ambush its prey.
- The female can store sperm for several years. She lays as many as 83 eggs, normally in a hole in sandy soil.

CREATED KIND MEMBERS

Alligator snapping turtle

CLASS:	Reptilia (reptiles)
ORDER:	Testudines (tortoises and turtles)
FAMILY:	Chelydridae (snapping turtles)
GENUS/SPECIES:	*Chelydra serpentina*
Size:	About 7–18 in (0.2–0.5 m)
Weight:	9–36 lbs (4–16 kg)
Original Diet:	Plants
Present Diet:	Fish, small mammals and birds, plants, and carrion
Habitat:	Fresh or brackish water bodies, preferably with muddy bottoms and abundant vegetation, from southern Canada to central Texas

COTTONMOUTH

COTTONMOUTH
CREATED ON DAY 6

DESIGN

Since the cottonmouth spends much of its time in the water, it needs to bask in the sun throughout the day to maintain a constant body temperature. Young cottonmouths flick their brightly-colored tail tips to attract frogs and small fish within their striking range.

FEATURES

- The cottonmouth is normally dark green, brown, or black. It has patterns of darker and lighter shades especially along its sides.
- The juvenile is brightly colored with reddish-brown crossbands on a brown background.
- The cottonmouth is also known as the water moccasin.

FUN FACTS

- The species name *piscivorus* actually means "fish-eater."
- The cottonmouth exposes its white mouth when threatened. This gives its predator warning.
- The cottonmouth is a pit viper. It possesses a pair of heat-sensing pits between its eyes and nostrils. The pits are able to detect temperature differences of as little as 0.05°C higher or lower than that of the background. This allows the snake to strike very accurately at the source of heat—its prey.

CREATED KIND MEMBERS

Rattlesnake, copperhead

CLASS:	Reptilia (reptiles)
ORDER:	Squamata (amphisbaenians, lizards, and snakes [scaly])
FAMILY:	Viperidae (pit vipers and vipers)
GENUS/SPECIES:	*Agkistrodon piscivorus*
Size:	20–48 in (51–121 cm)
Weight:	Nearly 2 lbs (0.9 kg)
Original Diet:	Plants
Present Diet:	Fish and other aquatic life; sometimes small mammals
Habitat:	Many varied aquatic regions of the southeastern U.S.

CROCODILE

CROCODILE
CREATED ON DAY 6

DESIGN

All crocodilians, including alligators, have a pouch in their throats that can block water from entering their throats when they eat underwater. Some believe that the crocodile species dates back to the time of the dinosaur. We would have to agree with this since both the crocodile kind and the dinosaurs were created on Day 6 of the Creation Week. The crocodile has eyes that are placed on top of its head, which allows it to see above water while its body is submerged.

FEATURES

- The crocodile is larger than the alligator and has a longer, more narrow snout.
- It has a streamlined body and webbed feet, which make it an efficient swimmer.

FUN FACTS

- The crocodile has taste buds, enabling it to taste its food. But it doesn't taste it very much since it swallow its food almost whole.
- After its young hatch, the mother croc will sometimes carry her young in her mouth to the water.
- The crocodile is the most advanced of all reptiles. Unlike other reptiles it has a four-chambered heart, a diaphragm and a cerebral cortex.

CREATED KIND MEMBERS

Alligator, caiman

CLASS:	Reptilia (reptiles)
ORDER:	Crocodylia (crocodiles, alligators, and relatives)
FAMILY:	Crocodylidae (crocodiles)
GENUS/SPECIES:	3 genera with 14 species
Size:	4–23 ft (1.2–7.1 m), depending on species
Weight:	Most 1,000 lbs (454 kg); some up to 2,000 lbs (907 kg)
Original Diet:	Plants
Present Diet:	Mammals, fish, reptiles, and even plants
Habitat:	Aquatic/Estuarine in the tropics of Africa, Asia, the Americas, and Australia

GALÁPAGOS TORTOISE

GALÁPAGOS TORTOISE
CREATED ON DAY 6

DESIGN

The shell of the tortoise is not solid; it is made of hollow structures that are like air chambers. This design gives the tortoise the ability to carry its shell without being crushed beneath its weight. The shell protects the lungs of the tortoise, which are located on top of the animal's body. However, if the tortoise is turned on its back, it may suffocate because its body could crush the lungs. The saddle-backed shell of some gives them a wider range of mobility, allowing the animal to reach up and get plants that are higher off the ground.

FEATURES

- Of the original 14 subspecies of Galápagos tortoises, three are extinct; the rest are endangered.
- These subspecies have different leg and neck lengths, shell shapes, and sizes.

FUN FACTS

- Yes, tortoises are slow. They move at just 0.2 mph (0.3 km/h).
- Male tortoises fight by stretching their necks as high as they can. The one with the highest reach wins.
- The Galápagos tortoise can pull its head, tail, and legs completely inside its shells, unlike a sea turtle.

CREATED KIND MEMBERS

Leopard tortoise, Indian star tortoise

CLASS:	Reptilia (reptiles)
ORDER:	Testudines (tortoises and turtles)
FAMILY:	Testudinidae (tortoises)
GENUS/SPECIES:	*Geochelone nigra*
Size:	Males: up to 6 ft (1.8 m); Females: 4–5 ft (1.2–1.5 m)
Weight:	Males: up to 575 lbs (260 kg); Females: 300 lbs (136 kg)
Original Diet:	Plants
Present Diet:	Cactus, fruits, vines, and grasses
Habitat:	Hot and dry islands and cooler, wetter islands within the Galápagos Islands

GILA MONSTER

GILA MONSTER
CREATED ON DAY 6

DESIGN

The Gila monster has the ability to consume large amounts of food at one time. This is necessary since it may not find food regularly in its desert environment. The Gila monster has powerful limbs for digging, a necessary design feature since this species is terrestrial and lives in dry desert regions and not in trees as many other lizards do.

FEATURES

- The Gila monster has short limbs; a short, flat tail; a heavy body; and black and pink, or yellow, scales.
- Fat can be stored in the tail and abdomen of the Gila monster to be utilized during the winter.

FUN FACTS

- The Gila monster is one of two kinds of venomous lizards. The venom is secreted through grooves in the teeth, and is used mainly for defense against predators.
- The Gila monster cannot jump.
- The female of this species lays 3–5 eggs in sandy soil, burrows, or under rocks.

CREATED KIND MEMBERS

Beaded lizard

CLASS:	Reptilia (reptiles)
ORDER:	Squamata (amphisbaenians, lizards, and snakes)
FAMILY:	Helodermatidae (venomous lizards)
GENUS/SPECIES:	*Heloderma suspectum*
Size:	Up to 2 ft (0.6 m)
Weight:	3–5 lbs (1.3–2.2 kg)
Original Diet:	Plants
Present Diet:	Birds, small mammals, lizards, and eggs
Habitat:	Desert and semiarid, shrubby regions in the Mohave, Sonoran, and Chihuahuan deserts of Southwest U.S. and into Mexico

INLAND BEARDED
DRAGON

INLAND BEARDED DRAGON
CREATED ON DAY 6

DESIGN

The inland bearded dragon searches for prey by perching on tall objects and watching for it. If food is scarce for a long period, it can remain dormant underground until conditions improve. If the dragon feels threatened, it will flare its throat and open its mouth to appear larger and more intimidating. These defense features were designed but were not necessary until after the Fall.

FEATURES

- This species is called "bearded" because the throat has a region that is flared when it is angry or excited, giving it a beard-like appearance.
- Most inland bearded dragons are brown or tan while some have patterns along their backs.

FUN FACTS

- The inland bearded dragon loves the sun. It will sunbathe for hours during the morning and afternoon.
- Smaller inland bearded dragons will "wave" at the more dominant male with one of their forelimbs.

CREATED KIND MEMBERS

Desert agama

CLASS:	Reptilia (reptiles)
ORDER:	Squamata (amphisbaenians, lizards, and snakes [scaly])
FAMILY:	Agamidae (Old Word reptiles)
GENUS/SPECIES:	*Pogona vitticeps*
Size:	16–22 in (0.4–0.6 m)
Weight:	10–18 oz (0.3–0.5 kg)
Original Diet:	Plants
Present Diet:	Animals, insects, and plants
Habitat:	Desert regions in central Australia

KING COBRA

KING COBRA
CREATED ON DAY 6

DESIGN

When the king cobra is scared or excited, it spreads the loose skin on its neck into the shape of a "hood." There are false eye spots on the hood, which probably serve to fool and/or scare potential predators. The female can keep the sperm of her mate for years, using it to impregnate herself several times. This design ensures that these animals can reproduce even if adult males are sparse. Right after the young hatch, the female king cobra abandons them.

FEATURES

- The adult king cobra is black, brown, green, or yellow with its throat being a lighter creamy color. The young are usually black with white or yellow markings.
- This species is most recognized by its hood that fans out when the snake is threatened or attacked.

FUN FACTS

- The king cobra can "hear" sounds even though it has no external ears or an eardrum. Sounds travel from the skin to the jaw muscle to the quadrate bone next to the ear bone, then to the inner ear. Its tongue brings odor molecules to its sensory Jacobson's organ.
- The king cobra is the largest venomous snake in the world.

CREATED KIND MEMBERS

Coral snake

CLASS:	Reptilia (reptiles)
ORDER:	Squamata (amphisbaenians, lizards, and snakes [scaly])
FAMILY:	Elapidae (cobras, coral snakes, and kraits)
GENUS/SPECIES:	*Ophiophagus hannah*
Size:	Average: 13 ft long (4 m)
Weight:	Up to 200 lbs (91 kg)
Original Diet:	Plants
Present Diet:	Lizards and other snakes
Habitat:	Grasslands and forests of India, southern China, and southeast Asia

KOMODO DRAGON

KOMODO DRAGON
CREATED ON DAY 6

DESIGN

When young, the Komodo dragon can live in trees where it eats mostly insects and birds. This gives the young protection from other, more aggressive males, which live on the gound. However, when it become older and heavier, it lives on the ground and eats mainly mammals, snakes, and fish. The Komodo dragon has very infectious bacteria in its mouth, which it uses to quickly bring down prey.

FEATURES

- The adult Komodo dragon is mostly green, gray, or black with white or yellow patches. This coloring helps it to be camouflaged in its environment.
- It is the world's largest lizard, out of over 3,000 lizard species.
- The Komodo has a huge muscular tail.

FUN FACTS

- The teeth of the Komodo dragon break easily. However, they are also frequently replaced.
- A pregnant female digs a nest chamber and buries her eggs in the dirt. Once they hatch, they must dig their way to the surface to survive.

CREATED KIND MEMBERS

Monitor lizard

CLASS:	Reptilia (reptiles)
ORDER:	Squamata (amphisbaenians, lizards, and snakes)
FAMILY:	Varanidae (monitor lizards)
GENUS/SPECIES:	*Varanus komodoensis*
Size:	Up to 10 ft (3 m)
Weight:	275 lbs (125 kg)
Original Diet:	Plants
Present Diet:	Mammals, birds, fish, snakes, and other Komodos
Habitat:	Forests and savannas, mainly on four Indonesian islands

NORTHERN
CORAL SNAKE

NORTHERN CORAL SNAKE
CREATED ON DAY 6

DESIGN

From the tip of its snout to just behind the eye, the head of the Northern coral snake is black. The tail is black and yellow, without any red rings. The Northern coral snake will swing or rattle its tail to confuse its predators. This feature did not become part of the animal's behavior until after the Fall, when it began to be hunted by other animals.

FEATURES

- The Northern coral snake is identified easily by its red, yellow, and black bands. However, it is often confused with a non-venomous milk snake with the same coloring, but different pattern. Remember the adage: Red on yellow, kill a fellow; red on black, venom-lack (or friend of Jack). Also remember that the head of this poisonous snake is black.

FUN FACTS

- This snake spends most of its time under the soil and only strikes at humans when it feels threatened.
- A coral snake has very short fangs so it bites its prey several times, twisting its head from side to side in order to squeeze venom into the wound.

CREATED KIND MEMBERS

Cobra

CLASS:	Reptilia (reptiles)
ORDER:	Squamata (amphisbaenians, lizards, and snakes [scaly])
FAMILY:	Elapidae (cobras, coral snakes, and kraits)
GENUS/SPECIES:	*Micrurus fulvius*; 5 subspecies
Size:	Average 20–30 in (51–76 cm)
Weight:	3–5 lbs (1.4–2.3 kg)
Original Diet:	Plants
Present Diet:	Mostly snakes; also lizards and frogs
Habitat:	Dry woods, scrub areas, and low wet areas in the southeastern U.S. and northeastern Mexico

POISON DART FROG

POISON DART FROG
CREATED ON DAY 6

DESIGN
In each species of the poison dart frog, once the tadpoles hatch, the parents carry them on their backs and deposit them in a pool of water or in the middle of a water-filled Bromeliad plant, the leaves of which are cup-shaped. These leaves capture the water of the rainforest and provide the perfect habitat for these developing young. How did these frogs know to do this? Simple, God designed them with that knowledge.

FEATURES
- The different species vary in color and size. Most species are bright orange, yellow, green, or red.
- Some species may also be non-toxic. These species are usually dull in color.

FUN FACTS
- Generally speaking, the brighter the color, the more toxic the organism.
- These frogs get their name "poison dart" because Indians rub the tips of their darts on the frog's back, which loads them with poison.
- In the wild, the frog's diet is the source of its skin toxins. Specimens kept in captivity are completely non-toxic.
- Another name for this frog is "poison arrow frog."

CREATED KIND MEMBERS
Rocket frog

CLASS:	Amphibia (cold-blooded vertebrate)
ORDER:	Anura (lack tails as adults)
FAMILY:	Dendrobatidae (poison dart frogs)
GENUS/SPECIES:	Well over 100 species
Size:	Up to 2.4 in (6 cm)
Weight:	Just ounces; varies within species
Original Diet:	Plants
Present Diet:	Insects
Habitat:	Rainforests of Central and South America

RATTLESNAKE

RATTLESNAKE
CREATED ON DAY 6

DESIGN

The rattlesnake is designed with hollow fangs. When the rattlesnake bites its victim, the lethal venom travels through these hollow fangs and is injected into the prey's body. Rattlesnake species inhabit many different regions. The genetic variation given to this original kind by God has enabled it to thrive in different areas.

FEATURES

- The most prominent feature of the rattlesnake is the rattle at the end of the tail. This rattle is made of a hard substance called keratin.
- Unlike some other snake species, the rattlesnake does not lay eggs; it gives birth to live young.

FUN FACTS

- When a rattlesnake molts, the scales at its end do not fall off; instead they become part of the rattle.
- The rattlesnake "smells" with its tongue. It flicks its tongue in and out, picking up odor particles from the ground and passing them over a special smelling organ in the roof of its mouth, called the Jacobson's organ.
- A rattlesnake uses its rattle to warn others of its presence. If you hear the sound of a rattle while in the woods, be careful where you step because a rattlesnake feels threatened.

CREATED KIND MEMBERS

Cottonmouth, copperhead

CLASS:	Reptilia (reptiles)
ORDER:	Squamata (amphisbaenians, lizards, and snakes [scaly])
FAMILY:	Viperidae (Old World vipers)
GENUS/SPECIES:	About 30 species in two genera (*Crotalus* and *Sistrurus*)
Size:	1–8 ft (0.6–2.4 m), depending on species
Weight:	3 oz–10 lbs (0.9–4.5 kg), depending on species
Original Diet:	Plants
Present Diet:	Small rodents and lizards
Habitat:	Desert, grasslands, and semi-arid regions of all the lower 48 U.S. states, and Central and South America

TOKAY GECKO

TOKAY GECKO
CREATED ON DAY 6

DESIGN

The tokay gecko smells using its nose and the Jacobson's organ, which is a pair of sacs lined with sensory cells in the palate. The tongue transports airborne molecules of scent to the Jacobson's organ. This gecko can leave its tail behind when a predator has hold of it. This part will continue to move while the lizard then escapes. This function probably developed after the Fall to help this species stay alive. Don't worry; it has the ability to regrow its tail. The feet of the gecko are specially designed to allow this creature to cling to almost any surface—from trees and leaves to ceilings and walls.

FEATURES

- The tokay gecko is the largest species of gecko today.
- It is often gray with bright red spots. It can lighten or darken its skin to provide camouflage for itself.

FUN FACTS

- You can see straight through the head of the tokay gecko by looking through its ears.
- A tokay gecko can unfold its skin to prevent its body from casting shadows on a tree.
- The name "tokay" comes from its courtship call: "to-kay, to-kay."

CREATED KIND MEMBERS

Golden gecko, crested gecko

CLASS:	Reptilia (reptiles)
ORDER:	Squamata (amphisbaenians, lizards, and snakes [scaly])
FAMILY:	Gekkonidae (geckos)
GENUS/SPECIES:	*Gekko gecko*
Size:	About 14 in (0.4 m)
Weight:	0.3–0.7 lbs (0.1–0.3 kg)
Original Diet:	Plants
Present Diet:	Insects, mice, and small lizards
Habitat:	Rainforests, mountainsides, rocky outcrops, and deserts of Southeast Asia

INDEX